THE ESSENTIAL
GIBRAN

About the Author

Kahlil Gibran, poet, philosopher, and artist, was born in 1883 in Bisharri, Lebanon, where he spent his early years. At the age of twelve he emigrated with his family to Boston and, after a period of study in Paris, he settled in New York. One of the world's most popular and influential writers, he is best known for his mystical writings, particularly *The Prophet*, a masterpiece that has been cited as the most widely read book of the twentieth century. His books have been translated into more than twenty languages and his paintings and drawings have been exhibited the world over.

THE ESSENTIAL
GIBRAN

Compiled and with an introduction
by Suheil Bushrui

KAHLIL GIBRAN

ONEWORLD

This edition published in 2013
First published by Oneworld Publications in 2007
Translation copyright © Suheil Bushrui 2007

ISBN: 978–1–85168–972–9
ebook ISBN: 978–1–78074–121–5

Typeset by Jayvee, Trivandrum, India
Printed and bound by
TJ International Ltd, Padstow, Cornwall, UK

Oneworld Publications
10 Bloomsbury Street
London WC1B 3SR
England
www.oneworld-publications.com

CONTENTS

~

PROLOGUE   ix
INTRODUCTION   x
CHRONOLOGY   xvi

SELECTIONS FROM GIBRAN'S ARABIC WORKS IN TRANSLATION

FROM *Music*   3
FROM *Nymphs of the Valley*   5
FROM *Spirits Rebellious*   15
FROM *The Broken Wings*   21
FROM *A Tear and a Smile*   24
FROM *The Processions*   39
FROM *The Tempests*   43
FROM *Beautiful and Rare Sayings*   56

SELECTIONS FROM GIBRAN'S ENGLISH WORKS

FROM *The Madman*   73

FROM *The Forerunner*   76

FROM *The Prophet*   80

FROM *Sand and Foam*   83

FROM *Jesus, the Son of Man*   86

FROM *The Earth Gods*   91

FROM *The Wanderer*   94

FROM *The Garden of the Prophet*   97

THREE LEBANESE FOLK POEMS TRANSLATED FROM THE ARABIC BY GIBRAN

O Mother Mine   103

I Wandered Among the Mountains   104

Three Maiden Lovers   105

SELECTIONS FROM THE LETTERS

Miscellaneous Letters   109

FROM *Letters to Ameen Rihani*   115

FROM *Letters to May Ziadah*   118

FROM *Letters to Mary Haskell*   127

OTHERS ON GIBRAN

GIBRAN: THE MAN   133

Mary Haskell   133
C F Bragdon   134
Juliet Thompson   134
Barbara Young   138

GIBRAN: THE POET   140

George Russell (AE)   140
Khalil S Hawi   141
Robert Hillyer   145
Mikhail Naimy   152
Francis Warner   157
Aïcha Lemsine Laïdi   158
Kathleen Raine   159

GIBRAN: THE ARTIST   160

Yusuf Huwayyik   160
Alice Raphael   160

EPILOGUE   175
BIBLIOGRAPHY   177
ACKNOWLEDGEMENTS   181

PROLOGUE

I shall live beyond death, and I shall sing in your ears
Even after the vast sea-wave carries me back
To the vast sea-depth.
I shall sit at your board though without a body,
And I shall go with you to your fields, a spirit invisible.
I shall come to you at your fireside, a guest unseen.
Death changes nothing but the masks that cover our faces.
The woodsman shall be still a woodsman,
The ploughman, a ploughman,
And he who sang his song to the wind shall sing it also to the
moving spheres.

Kahlil Gibran
The Garden of the Prophet

INTRODUCTION

"We have come together on this day not to glorify a dead man, but rather to be glorified in a living one."*

Mikhail Naimy

I N THE YEARS since his death in 1931, Kahlil Gibran has been confirmed as one of the most creative and controversial writers of the 20th century. His most famous book, *The Prophet*, which was published in 1923, has continued to capture the imagination of millions of people across the globe. When it was first published *The Prophet* sold 1,159 copies. In 1924, sales doubled. By the mid 1960s, the book had passed the two and a half million mark. By the mid 1980s and early 1990s, more than eight million copies had been sold. By all estimates *The Prophet* is without doubt among the most widely read books of the twentieth century, despite first appearing in an age when it was impossible to generate by intensive publicity the kind of sales which modern bestsellers enjoy.

---

* The opening address delivered in 1931 by Mikhail Naimy at the Fortieth Day Memorial Meeting held in Brooklyn.

In the early 1970s, Gibran's work began to be widely translated into different languages throughout the world. Today, Gibran's work is available in more than forty different languages, including some 'vernaculars' within the one language. This has enabled Gibran to be read and appreciated in places as far apart as Tokyo, Beijing, Delhi, Manila, Nairobi, Rome, Paris, London and New York.

In America, Gibran's standing as a hugely influential literary figure received dual confirmation in the academic and public spheres in the 1990s: the University of Maryland established the Kahlil Gibran Professorship under the auspices of the new Kahlil Gibran Research and Studies Project, and the United States Government created a memorial garden in his honour in the heart of Washington, D.C. The first was an institutional decision by a major American University, ending years of unwarranted academic reluctance to include Gibran in the curriculum. The second was the result of a bill passed by Congress and the House of Representatives, followed by a special commemoration ceremony in May 1991, over which the then President of the United States of America, George Bush, presided. Gibran must surely be the only immigrant poet ever to have been accorded such academic and national recognition.

* * *

Another important development in consolidating Gibran's position in the academic world was the First International Conference on Kahlil Gibran, which took place 9–12 December 1999.

The Kahlil Gibran Research and Studies Project at the University of Maryland organised this seminal conference on Kahlil Gibran, the first of its kind to be convened anywhere. The conference was unique in its format and content. Its principal purpose was to provide an opportunity for spirited dialogue on the legacy of Kahlil Gibran. More than merely a tribute and commemoration, the conference was also designed to help consolidate the pioneering academic activities of the Kahlil Gibran Research and Studies Project by developing close relations and collaborative activities with the Gibran National Committee in Lebanon. It was also appropriate that this conference was organised in partnership with UNESCO, in anticipation of the International Year of the Culture of Peace in the year 2000.

At this event, Gibran scholarship entered the international scene at the highest level, through collaboration with a wide range of partners, to advance a global movement towards a culture of peace. This international multicultural gathering drew more than 150 scholars, with representatives coming from Algeria, Australia, Canada, Egypt, England, France, Guadeloupe, Ireland, Jordan, Kuwait, Lebanon, the People's Republic of China, Syria, the United Arab Emirates, and the United States. Scholars, poets, writers, artists, and students came together not only to study Gibran's poetry, artwork, and vision of a global society, but also to initiate and develop definite plans for preserving Gibran's legacy by establishing a Gibran canon worthy of his exceptional accomplishment as a writer and artist. Such an international gathering was long overdue and the contribution of academic specialists and laypersons was essential to its success.

More recently, in 2006, the year which marks the seventy-fifth anniversary of Gibran's passing, a group of writers, scholars, artists, and critics, decided to form an International Association for the Study of the Life and Works of Kahlil Gibran. The goal of this association is to encourage the study of the life and works of Kahlil Gibran through conferences and newsletters, thereby circulating information about relevant events, courses, and publications. It is a landmark development in the history of Gibran scholarship, not only due to its international nature, but also because it is the first association to attempt to collect Gibran's entire literary and artistic output.

*   *   *

The Essential Gibran is a volume of selected passages, representative of Gibran's style and thought, which includes selections from his Arabic works, English works, letters, as well as selections from the body of scholarly criticism covering his work.

These selections offer a wide variety of theme, occasion, mood, and form. Reflective poetic prose, dramatic sketches, allegories and parables, national and international addresses, romantic writings of all kinds—these and more capture Gibran's essential style.

The essential Gibran is a universal figure whose profound humanity and concern for the highest standards of integrity in both a moral and literary sense transcends the boundaries between cultures that have too often found themselves opposed. This selection of passages offers a unique perspective of Kahlil Gibran as a poet of the culture of peace, and in many ways sheds new light on a twentieth century author who occupies a unique position in the pantheon of the world's great writers. The selections also provide an up-to-date re-evaluation of Gibran as a writer, critic, painter and thinker, and show how he assimilated and absorbed a multiplicity of influences in his Arabic and English writings, developing in the process a unique consciousness that transcends cultural barriers and still retains its potency today.

It is only too apparent how his abiding respect for universal human rights, promotion of the equality of men and women, and support for religious tolerance are pertinent today. His profound respect for the natural world, at a time when it was already under threat from the forces of industrialisation, makes him a pioneer of the ecological movement. Also emphasised in this work is a message of cultural, religious, and political reconciliation, which gains a particular poignancy and relevance in an age when East and West are in increasing need of mutual understanding to promote and strengthen a way towards peaceful coexistence.

Gibran's peaceful message found a voice in his new poetic vision, which appears in this new selection of passages from his English and Arabic writings. In his Arabic works, Gibran used the short narrative to express his ideas, but this was gradually replaced by the parable, the didactic essay, the aphorism, the allegory and the prose epigram, all of which became distinctive features of his English works. In both his English and Arabic works Gibran's peculiar style suggests a strong Biblical influence, reminiscent of the Song of Solomon and the Psalms, with strong echoes of Isaiah and the parables of Jesus. However, it was the prose poem which was his chosen vehicle of expression. According to the *Princeton Encyclopedia of Poetry and Poetics*, the prose poem is described as 'a composition able to have any or all features of the lyric except that it is put on the page ... as prose. It differs ... from free verse in that it has no line breaks from a short prose passage in that it has usually, more pronounced rhythm, sonorous effect, imagery and density of expression'. Such a form, relatively new in English at the time Gibran was writing, broke new ground in Arabic poetry.

Prose poetry perfectly suited Gibran's literary vision, central to which is the sense of 'an unseen order' behind visible things, an insight which C M Bowra identified in Blake, Coleridge, Wordsworth, Shelley and Keats—Gibran's Romantic predecessors. Gibran also identified this insight in his great Sufi masters, such as Ibn al-Farid, al-Ghazzali, Ibn al-'Arabi, and Rabi'a al-'Adawiyy'a. For Gibran, poetry was a universal language. In framing his own poetic diction he drew on sources of inspiration which spanned the traditions of East and West, writing in both English and Arabic. His Arabic writings above all bore the stamp of a Romanticism which, until Gibran's death, had never established itself as a cohesive movement in Arabic literature. The prose poem set him free from the shackles of restrictive verse techniques in English and Arabic and helped him to find his voice, a voice that was not only universal through the message he gave, but also through the form with which he chose to express himself.

Gibran's particular mystical vision cannot be adequately represented, as most Western critics demand, in the language of philosophy, or within the framework of materialistic logic. The recognition he has received so far has come from respectable and accomplished poets such as the Irishman AE (George Russell) and the American Robert Hillyer, both of whom have paid tribute to Gibran's unique genius, and have proposed for the purpose of correctly evaluating this type of literature, the adoption of a new critical methodology deriving from two separate cultural traditions, and bound by the prejudices and restrictions of neither. Perhaps the most recent recognition of the true stature of Gibran has come from Kathleen Raine, amongst the most respected of contemporary poets, and the most astute of literary critics. She wrote:

> Gibran was dismissed ... because of his immense following of ordinary men and women, for he answered to a deep need within the Western world, starved as it was of its spiritual food. Communism and Capitalism alike have believed that mankind could be fed on 'bread alone' but once again the prophets of the ever-living spirit have shown that the 'Word of God' is the necessary food of the soul. It is as if one mind had spoken through their several voices, none more eloquent or beautiful than the lonely voice of the Christian Lebanese Arab, Kahlil Gibran.

* * *

For this anthology, it was necessary to take a holistic approach to Gibran the man, the poet and the artist. Of course, any division of

Gibran's extensive work cannot be but inadequate and arbitrary to some degree, but it seemed most appropriate that this anthology should at least reflect not only the work of the poet himself but his relationships with others, and how others—whether contemporaries or not—saw him.

However, the scope of this anthology does not allow for an extensive survey of the significant scholarly work that has been published on Gibran in the last three decades. There are several major contributions to Gibran studies in both English and Arabic, the most outstanding of which is *Kahlil Gibran: His Life and World by Jean and Kahlil Gibran*, originally published in 1974. For a complete survey of Gibran scholarship between 1931 and 1989 see *Kahlil Gibran: Man and Poet*, by Suheil Bushrui and Joe Jenkins (Oxford, Oneworld, 1998 pp. 287–294).

* * *

As far as the transliteration of Arabic words is concerned, I have attempted to follow a uniform system, except in quoted passages, where the original transliteration is maintained. American forms of English orthography are used only when they occur in quoted passages.

CHRONOLOGY

1883   Gibran Kahlil Gibran was born on 6th January, near the Holy
       Cedar Grove on the edge of Wadi Qadisha (The Holy or
       Sacred Valley) in the town of Bisharri, Lebanon.

       His mother Kamileh, the daughter of a clergyman named
       Istiphan Rahme, was a widow when she married Khalil Gibran,
       his father. Kamileh's first husband was Hanna 'Abd-es-Salaam
       Rahmeh, by whom she had one son, Boutros, who was six years
       old when Gibran was born. Gibran's full name in Arabic was
       Gibran Khalil Gibran, the middle name being his father's. It is
       convention among Arabs to use the father's name after one's
       first name. Gibran always signed his full name in his Arabic
       works but dropped the first name in his English writings. He
       did this, and changed the correct spelling of 'Khalil' to 'Kahlil',
       at the instigation of his teacher of English at the Boston school
       he attended between 1895 and 1897.

1885   Miriana, Gibran's first sister, was born.

1887   Sultanah, Gibran's second sister, was born.

1895   Kahlil, his half-brother Boutros, his mother and his two sisters
       emigrated to the United States, settling in Boston's
       Chinatown, while his father remained in Lebanon.

1897   Gibran returned to Lebanon, where he began a course of inten-
       sive study at al-Hikmah School. He studied a variety of subjects

beyond those prescribed in the curriculum and devoted himself to the study of classical and contemporary Arabic literature.

1899 During the summer vacation at Bisharri, Gibran fell desperately in love with a beautiful young woman, whose identity remains a mystery. Gibran found his first love affair agonizing and exasperating. In the autumn, he returned to Boston, by way of Paris, and several years later described the unhappy affair in *Al-'Ajniha al-Mutakassirah* (The Broken Wings).

1902 Gibran returned to Lebanon, this time as a guide and interpreter to an American family but was forced to hurry back to Boston on hearing of the death of his sister, Sultanah and the serious illness of his mother.

1903 In March, his half-brother Boutros died, and his mother died in June, leaving Gibran and his sister Miriana in Boston.

1904 Gibran had begun to attract attention as an artist. Fred Holland Day, a well-known photographer, became his first patron, and in January, he held an exhibition at his studio of Gibran's paintings and drawings. In February, a second exhibition was held at the Cambridge School, a private educational institution owned and operated by Mary Haskell, who became Gibran's close friend. At the Cambridge School, he also met a beautiful and impulsive young woman of French origin, Emilie Michel (known as Micheline), with whom, it is said, he fell in love.

1905 Gibran published *Al-Musiqah* (Music), his first book in Arabic.

1906 Gibran published a savage attack against the established authority of the Church and State in *'Ara'is al-Muruj* (Nymphs of the Valley), which earned him the reputation of being a rebel and a revolutionary which was only partially mitigated by the publication of his later mystical and spiritual works.

1908 Besides arranging for the publication of *Al-'Arwah al-Mutamarridah* (Spirits Rebellious), Gibran also worked on *Falsafat al-Din wa'l-Tadayyun* (The Philosophy of Religion and Religiosity), which was never published. Through the generosity of Mary Haskell, who was determined to help him fulfill his ambition to become a great artist and thinker, he went to Paris, visiting London on the way, to study art at the *Academie Julien* and the *École des Beaux-Arts*. During his stay in Paris, he read the works of contemporary English and French writers and discovered a kindred spirit in the seventeenth-century English poet and painter, William Blake, whose influence on Gibran's thought and art was immense and lasting.

1909   Gibran continued his studies in Paris, where he met an old classmate from al-Hikmah, Yusuf Huwayyik, also an art student. The two became close friends but neither of them could subscribe to the principles of the modern movement in art and instead renewed their commitment to the values and principles of the classical tradition. Gibran rejected all that his teacher, *Maître* Lawrence, represented and eventually left him to work on his own. A brief meeting at the *Academie* with the French sculptor Auguste Rodin left an indelible impression on Gibran's mind.

Gibran's father died in Lebanon.

1910   Gibran, Ameen Rihani and Yusuf Huwayyik met in Paris and laid plans for the cultural renaissance of the Arab world. Among these was one, to which Rihani and Gibran gave form and shape during a visit to London. The plan called for the founding of an opera house in Beirut, the outstanding feature of which was to be two domes symbolising the reconciliation between Christianity and Islam.

After his return to Boston in October, Gibran proposed marriage to Mary Haskell, who was ten years his senior, but she gently advised him against such a union and decided not to marry him.

1911   At a time of intense political activity, occasioned by the freeing of Arab territories from Ottoman rule, Gibran founded *Al-Halaqa al-Dhahabiyyah* (The Golden Circle), one of many semi-political Arab societies which sprang up in Syria, Lebanon, Constantinople, Paris and New York. But the Golden Circle was not popular among Arab immigrants and was dissolved after the first meeting.

Gibran began to earn his living through portrait painting.

1912   Gibran moved from Boston to New York, where he hired a studio at 51 West Tenth Street, between Fifth and Sixth Avenue. 'The Hermitage', as Gibran called his studio, was to be his residence. He published *Al-'Ajniha al-Mutakassirah*, his autobiographical narrative, on which he had been working since 1903.

A literary and love relationship began between Gibran and May Ziadah, a Lebanese writer living in Egypt. Although they knew each other only through their correspondence, which lasted for more than twenty years, they achieved a rare intimacy and harmony of understanding, broken only by Gibran's death.

Gibran met 'Abdu'l-Bahá, the son of the founder of the Bahá'í Faith, who inspired Gibran's unique portrayal of Jesus in *Jesus, the Son of Man*. Gibran was so moved by 'Abdu'l-Bahá that he said, 'For the first time I saw form noble enough to be a receptacle for the Holy Spirit'.

1914   Gibran collected a number of prose poems which had appeared in different magazines since 1904 and published them under the title *Dam'ah wa Ibtisamah* (A Tear and a Smile).

In December, an exhibition of his paintings and drawings was held at the Montross Galleries, New York.

1917   Two exhibitions of Gibran's works were held at the Knoedler Galleries, New York and the Doll and Richards Galleries, Boston.

1918   Gibran published *The Madman*, his first book written in English.

1919   Gibran published *Twenty Drawings*, a collection of his drawings, with an introduction by Alice Raphael and *Al-Mawakib* (The Processions), a philosophical poem illustrated by Gibran himself which contains some of his best drawings.

1920   As well as publishing *Al-'Awasif* (The Tempests), a collection of short narratives and prose poems which had appeared in various Arabic journals between 1912 and 1918 and his second English book, *The Forerunner*, Gibran became founder-president of a literary society called *Al-Rabbitah al-Qalamiyah* (Arrabitah). This society, which included among its members distinguished Arab immigrants such as Iliya Abu Madi, Nasseeb Arida, Rasheed Ayoub, Wadi' Bahut, William Catzeflis, Abdul-Maseeh Haddad, Nadra Haddad and Mikhail Naimy, exerted a powerful influence on the work of immigrant Arab poets (*shu'ar' al-mahjar*) and successive generations of Arab writers.

1921   Gibran published a thematic 'play', *Iram Dhat al-'Imad* (Iram, City of Lofty Pillars), written in Arabic in the form of a discourse on mysticism.

Gibran's health began to deteriorate.

1922   In January, another exhibition of his work was held in Boston, this time at the Women's City Club.

1923   *Al-Badayi' wa al-Taray'if* (Beautiful and Rare Sayings), a selection of his Arabic works, was published in Cairo. This included his sketches (drawn from imagination when he was seventeen) of some of the greatest Arab philosophers and poets, such as ibn Sina (Avicenna), al-Ghazzali, al-Khansa', ibn al-Farid, Abu Nuwas, ibn al-Muqaffa'and others.

Gibran published *The Prophet*, his most successful work.

1926   Gibran published *Sand and Foam*, a book of aphorisms some of which were first written in Arabic and then translated into English.

1928   Gibran published *Jesus, the Son of Man*, his longest work.

1931   Two weeks before his death he published *The Earth Gods*.
Gibran died on Friday, 10th April, at St. Vincent's Hospital, New York, after a long and painful illness described in the post-mortem report as 'cirrhosis of the liver with incipient tuberculosis in one of the lungs'. His body lay in a funeral parlour for two days; thousands of admirers came to pay their last respects. His funeral service was conducted in Boston at the Church of our Lady of the Cedars, after which his body was returned to Lebanon, where it arrived, at the port of Beirut on 21st August. After a magnificent reception, unique in the history of Lebanon, Gibran's body was carried to Bisharri, to its final resting place in the old chapel of the Monastery of Mar Sarkis.

Not far from Mar Sarkis, a Gibran museum has been established by the Gibran National Committee of Bisharri. At his death, Gibran left two unpublished works which were published posthumously: the completed *Wanderer*, which appeared in 1932; and the unfinished *Garden of the Prophet*, which was completed and published in 1933 by Barbara Young, an American who claimed to have been Gibran's companion during the last seven years of his life.

SELECTIONS FROM GIBRAN'S ARABIC WORKS IN TRANSLATION

FROM *AL-MUSIQAH* (MUSIC)

1905

[*music*]

I sat by one whom my heart loves, and I listened to her words.
My soul began to wander in the infinite spaces where the
universe appeared like a dream, and the body like a narrow
prison.

The enchanting voice of my Beloved entered my heart.

This is Music, oh friends, for I heard her through the sighs of
the one I loved, and through the words, half-uttered
between her lips.

With the eyes of my hearing I saw my Beloved's heart.

My friends: Music is the language of spirits. Its melody is like
the frolicsome breeze that makes the strings quiver with
love. When the gentle fingers of Music knock at the door
of our feelings, they awaken memories that have long lain
hidden in the depths of the Past. The sad strains of Music
bring us mournful recollections; and her quiet strains bring
us joyful memories. The sound of strings makes us weep at
the departure of a dear one, or makes us smile at the peace
God has bestowed upon us.

The soul of Music is of the Spirit, and her mind is of the
Heart.

When God created Man, he gave him Music as a language different from all other languages. And early man sang her glory in the wilderness; and she drew the hearts of kings and moved them from their thrones.

Our souls are like tender flowers at the mercy of the winds of Destiny. They tremble in the morning breeze, and bend their heads under the falling dews of heaven.

The song of the bird awakens Man from his slumber and invites him to join in the psalms of glory to Eternal Wisdom that has created the song of the bird.

Such music makes us ask ourselves the meaning of the mysteries contained in ancient books.

Translated by A R Ferris

FROM '*ARA'IS AL-MURUJ*
(NYMPHS OF THE VALLEY)

1906

Dust of the ages and the eternal fire

I Autumn, 116 BC

THE NIGHT was still and all life slept in the City of the Sun.* The lamps in the houses scattered around the great temples in the midst of olive and laurel trees had long been extinguished. The rising moon spilled its rays over the whiteness of the tall marble columns which stood upright like giant sentinels in the tranquil night over the shrines of the gods. They looked in wonder and awe toward the towers of Lebanon, dwelling in rugged places on distant heights.

At that magic hour poised between the spirits of the sleeping and the dreams of the infinite, Nathan, son of the priest, entered the temple of Astarte.† He carried in his trembling hand a torch and kindled with it the lamps and the censers. The sweet smell of frankincense and myrrh rose in the air, and the image of the goddess was adorned with a delicate veil

---

* Baalbek, city of Baal, the sun god. The ancients knew it as Heliopolis, and its ruins still stand in the vicinity of the new city of Baalbek in Lebanon.
† Goddess of love and beauty among the ancient Phoenicians, who worshipped her in Tyre, Sidon, Byblos, and Baalbek. The Greek Aphrodite and the Roman Venus.

like the veil of desire and longing that enshrines the human heart. He prostrated himself before an altar overlaid with ivory and gold, raised his hands in supplication, and lifted his eyes with tears to the heavens. In a voice strangled with grief and broken by harsh sobs, he cried:

'Mercy, O great Astarte. Mercy, O goddess of love and beauty. Have pity on me and lift the hand of death from my beloved, whom my soul has chosen to do your will. The potions and powders of the physicians have availed nothing, and the charms of the priests and wise men are in vain. There remains but your sacred name to help and succour me. Answer, then, my prayer; look to my contrite heart and agony of spirit, and let her that is the part of my soul live so that we may rejoice in the secrets of your love and exult in the beauty of youth, which proclaims your glory ... From the depths do I cry unto you, sacred Astarte. From out of the darkness of this night do I seek the protection of your mercy ... Hear my cry! I am your servant Nathan, son of Hiram the priest, who has dedicated his life to the service of your altar. I love a maiden and have taken her for my own, but the brides of the Jinn have breathed upon her beautiful body the breath of a strange disease. They have sent the messenger of death to lead her to their enchanted caves. He now lies like a roaring hungry beast by her couch, spreading his black wings over her and stretching out his defiled hands to wrest her from me. Because of this I have come to you. Take pity on me and let her live. She is a flower that has not lived to enjoy the summer of its life; a bird whose joyful song greeting the dawn is cut off. Save her from the clutches of death and we will sing praises and make burnt offerings to the glory of your name. We will bring sacrifices to your altar and fill your vessels with wine and sweet-scented oil and spread your tabernacle with roses and jasmine. We will burn incense and sweet-smelling aloes wood before your image .... Save her, O goddess of miracles, and let love conquer death, for you are the mistress of love and death'.

He stopped speaking, weeping and sighing in his agony. Then he continued: 'Alas, sacred Astarte, my dreams are shattered and the last breath of my life is ebbing; my heart is dying within me and my eyes are burned with tears. Sustain me through your compassion and let my beloved remain with me'.

At that moment one of his slaves entered, came slowly towards him, and whispered in his ear: 'She has opened her eyes, my lord, and looks round her couch but does not see you. I come to call you, for she cries for you continually'.

Nathan rose and went out quickly, the slave following. On reaching his palace he entered the room of the sick girl and stood over her bed. He took her thin hand in his and kissed her lips repeatedly as though he would breathe new life into her emaciated body. She turned her face, which had been hidden among the silken pillows, towards him and opened her eyes a little. Upon her lips appeared the shadow of a smile – all that remained of life in her beautiful body; the last ray of light from a departing spirit; the echo from the cry of a heart fast approaching its end. She spoke, and her breath came in short gasps like that of a starving child.

'The gods call me, betrothed of my soul, and Death has come to part us .... Grieve not, for the will of the gods is sacred and the demands of Death are just .... I am going now, but the twin cups of love and youth are still full in our hands and the ways of sweet life lie before us ... I am going, my beloved, to the meadows of the spirits, but I shall return to this world. Astarte brings back to this life the souls of lovers who have gone to the infinite before they have tasted of the delights of love and the joys of youth .... We shall meet again, Nathan, and together drink of the morning dew from the cups of the narcissus and rejoice in the sun with the birds of the fields .... Farewell, my beloved'.

Her voice grew low and her lips began to tremble like the petals of a flower before the dawn breeze. Her lover clasped her to him, wetting her neck with his tears. When his lips touched her mouth they found it cold like ice. He gave a terrible cry, rent his garments, and threw himself upon her dead body, while his spirit in its agony hovered between the deep sea of life and the abyss of death.

In the stillness of that night the eyelids of those who slept trembled, the women of the quarter grieved, and the souls of children were afraid, for the darkness was rent by loud cries of mourning and bitter weeping rising from the palace of Astarte's priest. When morning came the people sought Nathan to console him and soothe him in his affliction, but they did not find him.

Many days later, when the caravan from the east arrived, its leader related how he had seen Nathan far off in the wilderness wandering like a stricken soul with the gazelles of the deserts.

Centuries passed and the feet of time obliterated the work of the ages. The gods went from the land, and other gods came in their stead – gods of anger wedded to destruction and ruin. They razed the fine temple of the City of the Sun and destroyed its beautiful palaces. Its verdant gardens became dry, and drought overtook its fertile fields. Nothing remained in that valley except decaying ruins to haunt the memory with ghosts of yesterday and recall the faint echo of psalms chanted to a past glory. But the ages that pass on and sweep away the works of man cannot destroy his dreams, nor can they weaken his innermost feelings and emotions; for these endure as long as the immortal spirit. Here, perhaps, they are concealed; there they may go into hiding like the sun at eventide or the moon with the approach of the morning.

II. Spring, AD 1890

D AY WAS waning and the light was fading as the sun gathered up her garments from the plains of Baalbek. Ali Al-Husaini‡ turned with his flock towards the ruins of the temple and sat down by the fallen pillars. They looked like ribs of a long-forgotten soldier that had been broken in battle and rendered naked by the elements. The sheep gathered around him browsing, lulled into safety by the melodies of his pipe.

Midnight came and the heavens cast the seeds of the morrow into its dark depths. The eyelids of Ali grew tired with the spectres of wakefulness. His mind became weary with the passing of the processions of imagination marching through the awful silence amidst the ruined walls. He supported himself on his arm while sleep crept upon him and covered his wakefulness lightly with the folds of its veil as the fine mist touches the surface of a calm lake.

Forgotten was his earthly self as he met his spiritual self; his hidden self filled with dreams transcending the laws and teachings of men. A vision appeared before his eyes and things hidden revealed themselves to him. His spirit stood apart from the procession of time ever hurrying on toward nothingness. It stood alone before the serried ranks of thoughts and contending emotions. He knew, or he was about to

‡ The Husainis are an Arab tribe who used to dwell in tents around Baalbek.

know, for the first time in his life, the causes of this spiritual hunger overtaking his youth. A hunger uniting all the bitterness and sweetness in existence. A thirst bringing together a cry of yearning and the serenity of fulfilment. A longing that all the glory of this world cannot blot out nor the course of life conceal.

For the first time in his life Ali Al-Husaini felt a strange sensation awakened in him by the ruins of the temple. A feeling without form of the remembrance of incense from the censers. A haunting feeling that played unceasingly upon his senses as the finger-tips of a musician play upon the strings of his lute. A new feeling welled up from out of nothingness – or perhaps it was from something. It grew and developed until it embraced the whole of his spiritual being. It filled his soul with an ecstasy near to death in its kindness, with a pain sweet in its bitterness, agreeable in its harshness. A feeling born of the vast spaces of a minute filled with sleepiness. A minute that gave birth to the patterns of the ages as the nations grow from one seed.

Ali looked toward the ruined shrine, and his weariness gave place to an awakening of the spirit. The ruined remains of the altar appeared to his sight and the places of the fallen pillars and the foundations of the crumbling walls grew clear and sharp. His eyes became glazed and his heart beat violently, and then suddenly, as with one who was until then sightless, the light returned to his eyes and he began to see – and he thought and reflected. And out of the chaos of thought and the confusion of reflection were born the phantoms of memory, and he remembered. He remembered those pillars standing upright in greatness and pride. He recalled the silver lamps and censers surrounding the image of an awe-inspiring goddess. He recalled the venerable priests laying their offerings before an altar overlaid with ivory and gold. He recalled the maidens beating their tambourines and the youths chanting praises to the goddess of love and beauty. He remembered, and saw these figures becoming clear before his gaze. He felt the impressions of sleeping things stirring in the silences of his depths. But remembrance brings back naught save shadowy forms, which we see from the past of our lives; neither does it bring back to our ears except the echoes of voices that they once heard. What then was the link joining these haunting memories to the past life of a youth reared among the tents, who passed the springtime of his life tending his sheep in the wilderness?

Ali rose and walked among the ruins and broken stones. Those distant remembrances raised the covering of forgetfulness from his mind's eyes as a woman brushes away a cobweb from the glass of her mirror. And so it was until he reached the heart of the temple and then stood still as though a magnetic attraction in the earth were drawing his feet. And then he suddenly saw before him a broken statue lying on the ground. Involuntarily he prostrated himself before it. His feelings overflowed within him like the flowing of blood from an open wound; his heartbeats rose and fell, like the rise and fall of sea waves. He was humbled in its sight and he sighed a bitter sigh and wept in his grief, for he felt an aloneness that wounded and a distance that annihilated, separating his spirit from the beautiful spirit that was by his side ere he entered this life. He felt his very essence as naught save part of a burning flame that God had separated from his self before the beginning of time. He felt the light fluttering of wings in his burning bones, and around the relaxed cells of his brain a strong and mighty love taking possession of his heart and soul. A love that revealed the hidden things of the spirit to the spirit, and by its actions separated the mind from the regions of measurement and weight. A love that we hear speaking when the tongues of life are silent; that we behold standing as a pillar of fire when darkness hides all things. That love, that god, had fallen in this hour upon the spirit of Ali Al-Husaini and awakened in it feelings bitter and sweet as the sun brings forth the flowers side by side with thorns.

What thing is this love? Whence does it come? What does it want of a youth resting with his flock among the ruined shrines? What is this wine which courses through the veins of one whom maidens' glances left unmoved? What are these heavenly melodies that rise and fall upon the ears of a bedouin who heard not yet the sweet songs of women?

What thing is this love and whence does it come? What does it want of Ali, busied with his sheep and his flute away from men? Is it something sown in his heart by man-wrought beauties without the awareness of his senses? Or is it a bright light veiled by the mist and now breaking forth to illumine the emptiness of his soul? Is it perchance a dream come in the stillness of the night to mock at him, or a truth that was and will be to the end of time?

Ali closed his tear-filled eyes and stretched out his hands like a beggar seeking pity. His spirit trembled within him, and out of its trembling came broken sobs in which were both whining complaint and the fire of longing. In a voice that only the faint sound of words lifted above a sigh he called:

'Who are you that are so close to my heart yet unseen by my eyes, separating myself from my self, linking my present to distant and forgotten ages? Are you a nymph, a sprite, come from the world of immortals to speak to me of the vanity of life and the frailty of the flesh? Are you mayhap the spirit of the queen of the Jinn risen from the bowels of the earth to enslave my senses and make of me a laughing-stock among the young men of my tribe? Who are you and what thing is this temptation, quickening and destroying, which has seized hold of my heart? What feelings are these that fill me with fire and light? Who am I and what is this new self I call "I" yet which is a stranger to me? Is the spring water of life swallowed up with the particles of air and I am become an angel that sees and hears all things secret? Am I drunk of the Devil's brew and become blinded to real things?'

He fell silent for a little while. His emotion grew in strength and his spirit grew in stature. He spoke again:

'O one whom the spirit reveals and brings near and whom the night conceals and makes distant; O beautiful spirit hovering in the spaces of my dreams, you have awakened within my being feelings that were aslumber like flower seeds hidden beneath the snow, and passed as the breeze, the bearer of the breath of the fields. And touched my senses so that they are shaken and disturbed as the leaves of a tree. Let me look upon you, if you be then of body and substance. Command sleep to close my eyelids that I might see you in my dreaming, if you be free of the earth. Let me touch you; let me hear your voice. Tear aside the veil that covers my whole being and destroy the fabric that conceals my divineness. Grant me wings that I might fly after you to the regions of the assembly on high, if you be of those that inhabit there. Touch with magic my eyelids and I shall follow you to the secret places of the Jinn, if you be one of their nymphs. Put your unseen hand upon my heart and possess me, if you be free to let follow whom you will.'

So did Ali whisper into the ears of darkness words moving up from the echo of a melody in the depths of his heart. Between his vision and his surroundings flowed phantoms of the night as though they were incense rising out of his hot tears. Upon the walls of the temple appeared enchanted pictures in the colours of the rainbow.

So passed the hour. He rejoiced in his tears and was glad in his grief. He listened to the beating of his heart. He looked to beyond all things as though seeing the pattern of this life slowly fading and in its place a dream wonderful in its beauties, awful in its thought-images. As a prophet who looks to the stars of the heavens watching for divine inspiration, so he awaited the coming of the minutes. His quick sighing stopped his quiet breathing and his spirit forsook him to hover around him and then return as though it were seeking among those ruins a lost loved one.

The dawn broke and the silence trembled at the passing of the breeze. The vast spaces smiled the smiles of a sleeper who has seen in his sleep the image of his beloved. The birds appeared from clefts in the ruined walls and moved about among the pillars, singing and calling out one to the other and heralding the approach of day. Ali rose to his feet and put his hand to his hot brow. He looked about him with dull eyes. Then like Adam when his eyes were opened by the breath of God, he looked at all before him and wondered. He approached his sheep and called them; they rose and shook themselves and trotted quietly behind him toward the green pastures.

Ali walked on before his flock, his large eyes looking into the serene atmosphere. His inmost feelings took flight from reality to reveal to him the secrets and closed things of existence; to show him that which had passed with the ages and that which yet remained, as it were in one flash; and in one flash to make him forget it all and bring back to him his yearning and longing. And he found between himself and the spirit of his spirit a veil like a veil between the eye and the light. He sighed, and with his sigh was a flame stripped from his burning heart.

He came to the brook whose babblings proclaimed the secrets of the fields, and he sat him down on its bank beneath a willow tree whose boughs hung down into the water as though they would suck up its sweetness. The sheep cropped the grass with bent heads, the morning dew gleaming on the whiteness of their wool.

After the passing of a minute Ali began to feel the swift beating of his heart and the renewed quaking of his spirit. Like a sleeper whom the sun's rays have startled into wakefulness he moved and looked about him. He beheld a girl coming out from among the trees carrying a jar upon her shoulder. Slowly she walked towards the water; her bare feet were wet with dew. When she came to the edge of the stream and bent to fill her jar she looked toward the opposite bank and her eyes met the eyes of Ali. She gave a cry and threw the jar to the ground and drew back a little. It was the act of one who finds an acquaintance who has been lost.

A minute passed by and its seconds were as lamps lighting the way between their two hearts, creating from the silence strange melodies to bring back to these two the echo of vague remembrances, and show to each one the other in another place, surrounded by shadows and figures, far from that stream and those trees. The one looked at the other with imploring in the eyes of each; and each found favour in the eyes of the other; each listened to the sighing of the other with ears of love.

They communed, the one with the other, in all the tongues of the spirit. And when full understanding and knowledge possessed their two souls, Ali crossed the stream, drawn thither by an invisible power. He drew nigh to the girl, embraced her, and kissed her lips and her neck and her eyes. She made no movement in his arms, as though the sweetness of the embrace had robbed her of her will and the lightness of touch taken from her all strength. She yielded as the fragrance of the jasmine gives itself up to the currents of air. She dropped her head upon his breast like one exhausted who has found rest, and sighed deeply. A sigh telling of the birth of contentment in a constricted heart and the stirring of life within that had been sleeping and was now awakened. She raised her head and looked into his eyes, the look of one who despises the speech customary among men by the side of silence – the language of the spirit; the look of one who is not content that love should be a soul in a body of words.

The two lovers walked among the willow trees, and the oneness of each was a language speaking of the oneness of both, an ear listening in silence to the inspiration of love, and a seeing eye seeing the glory of happiness. The sheep followed them, eating the tops of flowers and herbs, and the birds met them from all sides with songs of enchantment.

When they came to the end of the valley, by which time the sun had risen and cast upon the heights a golden mantle, they sat down by a rock that protected the violets with its shadow. After a time the girl looked into the black eyes of Ali while the breeze played in her hair as though it were invisible lips that would kiss her. She felt bewitched fingertips caressing her tongue and lips, and her will was a prisoner. She spoke and said in a voice of wounding sweetness:

'Astarte has brought back our souls to this life so that the delights of love and the glory of youth might not be forbidden us, my beloved.'

Ali closed his eyes, for the music of her words had made clear the patterns of a dream that he saw oft-times in his sleep. He felt that unseen wings were bearing him away from that place to a room of strange form. He was standing by the side of a couch on which lay the body of a beautiful woman whose beauty death had taken with the warmth of her lips. He cried out in his anguish at this terrible scene. Then he opened his eyes and found sitting beside him the maiden; upon her lips was a smile of love and in her glance the rays of life. His face lighted up and his spirit was refreshed, the visions were scattered and he forgot both the past and the future ....

The lovers embraced and drank of the wine of kisses until they were satisfied. They slept each enfolded in the arms of the other until the shade moved away and the sun's heat awakened them.

Translated by H M Nahmad

FROM *AL-'ARWAH AL-MUTAMARRIDAH* (SPIRITS REBELLIOUS)

1908

From a speech by Khalil the heretic

From the depths of these depths
We call you, O Liberty – hear us!
From the corners of this darkness
We raise our hands in supplication – turn your gaze towards
    us!
On the expanse of these snows
We lay ourselves prostrate before you, have compassion upon
    us!

We stand now before your terrible throne
Wearing the blood-smeared garments of our fathers;
Covering our heards with the dust of the tombs mingled with
    their remains;
Drawing the swords which have been sheathed in their entrails;
Raising the spears that have pierced their breasts;
Dragging the chains that have withered their feet;

Crying aloud cries that have wounded their throats,
And lamentations that have filled the darkness of their
    prisons;
Praying prayers that have sprung out of the pain of their hearts –
Listen, O Liberty, and hear us!

From the sources of the Nile to the estuary of the Euphrates
The wailing of souls surging with the scream of the abyss rises;
From the frontiers of the peninsula to the mountains of
    Lebanon
Hands are outstretched to you, trembling in the agony of death;
From the coast of the gulf to the ends of the desert
Eyes are uplifted to you with pining hearts –
Turn, O Liberty, and look upon us.

In the corners of huts standing in the shadow of poverty and
    humiliation,
Breasts are being beaten before you;
In the emptiness of houses erected in the darkness of ignor-
    ance and folly,
Hearts are cast before you;
And in the corners of houses buried in the clouds of oppres-
    sion and tyranny,
Spirits are longing for you –
Look upon us, O Liberty, and have compassion.

In schools and offices
Despairing youth calls upon you;
In the churches and mosques
The forsaken book invites you;
In the councils and courts
The neglected law implores you –
Have pity, O Liberty, and save us.

In our narrow streets
The merchant barters his days only to pay the thieves from the
    West,
And none is there to advise him!
In our barren fields

The peasant ploughs the earth with his finger-nails,
And sows the seeds of his heart and waters them with his tears,
And nothing does he harvest save thorns and thistles,
And none is there to teach him!
In our empty plains
The Bedouin walks bare-foot, naked and hungry
And none is there to have mercy upon him –
Speak, O Liberty, and teach us ...

From the very beginning the darkness of the
night has descended upon our souls –
How long until the dawn?
From prison to prison our bodies move, and the mocking ages
    pass us by –
How long are we to bear the mockery of the ages?
From yoke to heavier yoke our necks do pass
And the nations of the earth look at us and laugh –
How long shall we endure the mockery of nations?
From fetters to fetters our path leads us
And neither do the fetters disappear nor do we perish –
How long shall we remain alive? ...

From the grasp of Pharaoh
To the claws of Nebuchadnezzar;
To the nails of Alexander;
To the swords of Herod;
To the claws of Nero;
To the fangs of the devil;
Whose yoke is going to enslave us now?
And when shall we fall within the grasp of death to find com-
    fort away from the silence of non-existence?

With the strength of our arms they erected the pillars of their
    temples and shrines to glorify their gods;
On our backs they brought clay and stones to build castles to
    strengthen their strongholds;
And with the power of our bodies they built pyramids to
    render their names immortal;

How long are we to build castles and palaces
And live but in huts and caves?
How long are we to fill granaries and stores
And eat nothing but garlic and clover?
How long are we to weave silk and wool
And be clad in tattered cloth?

Through their cunning and treachery they have set clan
against clan;
Have separated group from group;
Have sown the seeds of hate twixt tribe and tribe –
How long are we then to wither like ashes before this cruel
hurricane,
And fight like hungry young lions near this stinking carcass?

In order to secure their power and to rest at their heart's ease
they have armed the Durzi to fight the Arab;
Have instigated the Shi'i against the Sunni;
Have incited the Kurd to slaughter the Bedouin;
Have encouraged the Mohammadan to fight the Christian –
How long is a brother to fight his brother on the breast of the
mother?
How long is a neighbour to threaten his neighbour near the
tomb of the beloved?
How long are the Cross and the Crescent to remain apart
before the eyes of God?

Listen, O Liberty, and harken unto us.
Turn your gaze towards us, O mother of the earth's inhabitants,
For we are not the offspring of your rival;
Speak with the tongue of any one of us
For from one spark the dry straw catches fire;
Awaken with the sound of your wings the spirit of one of our
men
For from one cloud one lightning flash illuminates valley-
lanes and mountain-tops.
Disperse with your resolve these dark clouds;
Descend as a thunderbolt,

Destroy like a catapult
The props of those thrones erected on bones and skulls,
Plated with the gold of taxes and bribery
And soaked in blood and tears.

Listen to us, O Liberty,
Have compassion on us, O Daughter of Athens,
Rescue us, O Sister of Rome,
Save us, O Companion of Moses,
Come to our aid, O beloved of Mohammad,
Teach us, O bride of Jesus,
Strengthen our hearts that we may live;
Or strengthen the arms of our enemies against us
That we may wither, perish and find peace.

Translated by S B Bushrui

FROM *AL-'AJNIHA AL-MUTAKASSIRAH*
(THE BROKEN WINGS)

1912

Poets of the West think of Lebanon as a legendary place, forgotten since the passing of David and Solomon and the Prophets, as the Garden of Eden became lost after the fall of Adam and Eve. To those Western poets, the word 'Lebanon' is a poetical expression associated with a mountain whose sides are drenched with the incense of the Holy Cedars. It reminds them of the temples of copper and marble standing stern and impregnable and of a herd of deer feeding in the valleys. That night I saw Lebanon dream-like with the eyes of a poet ....

It was midnight, and we could see the crescent moon rising from behind Mount Sunnin, and it looked, in the midst of the stars, like the face of a corpse, in a coffin surrounded by the dim lights of candles. And Lebanon looked like an old man whose back was bent with age and whose eyes were a haven for insomnia, watching the dark and waiting for dawn, like a king sitting on the ashes of his throne in the debris of his palace.

The mountains, trees, and rivers change their appearance with the vicissitudes of times and seasons, as a man changes with his experiences and emotions. The lofty poplar that resembles a bride in the daytime, will look like a column of smoke in the evening; the huge rock that stands impregnable at noon, will appear to be a miserable pauper at night, with earth for his bed and the sky for his cover; and the rivulet that we see glittering in the morning and hear singing the hymn of Eternity, will, in the evening, turn to a stream of tears wailing like a mother bereft of her child, and Lebanon, that had looked dignified a week before, when the moon was full and our spirits were happy, looked sorrowful and lonesome that night ....

Why do I occupy these pages with words about the betrayers of poor nations instead of reserving all the space for the story of a miserable woman with a broken heart? Why do I shed tears for oppressed peoples rather than keep all my tears for the memory of a weak woman whose life was snatched by the teeth of death?

But my dear readers, don't you think that such a woman is like a nation that is oppressed by priests and rulers? Don't you believe that thwarted love which leads a woman to the grave is like the despair which pervades the people of the earth? A woman is to a nation as light is to a lamp. Will not the light be dim if the oil in the lamp is low? ...

The most beautiful word on the lips of mankind is the word 'Mother', and the most beautiful call is the call of 'My mother'. It is a word full of hope and love, a sweet and kind word coming from the depths of the heart. The mother is everything – she is our consolation in sorrow, our hope in misery, and our strength in weakness. She is the source of love, mercy, sympathy, and forgiveness. He who loses his mother loses a pure soul who blesses and guards him constantly ....

Our conversation was not limited to love; every now and then we drifted on to current topics and exchanged ideas. During the course of conversation Selma spoke of woman's place in society, the imprint that the past generation had left on her character, the relationship between husband and wife, and the spiritual diseases and corruption which threatened married life. I remember her saying: 'The poets and writers are trying to understand the reality of woman, but up to this day they have not understood the hidden secrets of her heart, because they look upon her from behind the sexual veil and see nothing but externals; they look upon her through a magnifying glass of hatefulness and find nothing except weakness and submission'.

On another occasion she said, pointing to the carved pictures on the walls of the temple, 'In the heart of this rock there are two symbols depicting the essence of a woman's desires and revealing the hidden secrets of her soul, moving between love and sorrow – between affection and sacrifice, between Ishtar sitting on the throne and Mary standing by the cross. The man buys glory and reputation but the woman pays the price' ....

'... Let us leave this country and all its slavery and ignorance for another country far away and unreached by the hands of thieves. Let us go to the coast under the cover of night and catch a boat that will take us across the oceans, where we can find a new life full of happiness and understanding. Do not hesitate, Selma, for these minutes are more precious to us than the crowns of kings and more sublime than the thrones of angels. Let us follow the column of light that leads us from this arid desert into the green fields where flowers and aromatic plants grow'.

Translated by A R Ferris

FROM *DAM'AH WA IBTISAMAH*
(A TEAR AND A SMILE)

1914

Letters of fire

Here lies one whose name was writ in water.

John Keats

Is it that the nights pass by us
And destiny treads us underfoot?
Is it thus the ages engulf us and remember us not save as a
    name upon a page writ in water in place of ink?
Is this life to be extinguished
And this love to vanish
And these hopes to fade?

Shall death destroy that which we build,
And the winds scatter our words
And darkness hide our deeds?

Is this then life?
A past that has gone and left no trace,
A present, pursuing the past?

Or a future, without meaning, save when it is present and past?
Shall all that is joy in our hearts
And all that saddens our spirit
Vanish ere we know their fruits?

Shall man be even as the foam
That sits an instant on the ocean's face
And is taken by the passing breeze –
And is no more?

No, in truth, for the verity of life is life;
Life whose birth is not in the womb
Nor its end in death.

What are these years if not an instant in Eternity?

This earthly life and all therein
Is but a dream by the side of the awakening we call by death
   and terror.
A dream, yet all we see and do therein
Endures with God's enduring.

The air bears every smile and every sigh
Arising from our hearts,
And stores away the voice of every kiss
Whose source and spring is Love.
And angels make account
Of every tear dropped by sadness from our eyes,
And fill the ears of wandering spirits
With song created by our hidden joys.

Yonder in the Hereafter
We shall see the beating of our hearts
And comprehend the meaning of our godlike state
That in this day we hold as naught
Because despair is ever at our heels.

The erring that today we call a weakness
Shall appear on the morrow
A link in man's existence.

The fret and toil that requite us not
Shall abide with us to tell our glory.

The afflictions that we bear
Shall be to us a crown of honour.

* * *

If that sweet singer Keats had known that his songs would
    never cease to plant the love of beauty in men's hearts,
    surely he had said:
'Write upon my grave stone: Here lie the remains of him who
    wrote his name on Heaven's face in letters of fire'.

Translated by H M Nahmad

The abode of happiness

MY HEART was weary within me and bade me farewell and
repaired to the Abode of Happiness. And when it was come
to that sanctuary which the spirit had sanctified, it stood in
wonderment, for it saw not there things it had imagined.

It saw not there power or wealth, nor yet authority. It saw naught
save the youth of Beauty and his companion the daughter of Love and
their child Wisdom.

Then my heart spoke to the daughter of Love and said: 'Where is
contentment, O Love? I had heard that it shared with you this
dwelling'. And she answered: 'Contentment is away preaching in the
city, where is corruption and greed; we are not in need of it in this place.
Happiness desires not contentment, for happiness is naught but a
longing which union embraces; contentment is a diversion conquered
by forgetfulness. The immortal soul is not contented, for it is ever
desiring of perfection; and perfection is the Infinite'.

And my heart spoke to the youth of Beauty and said: 'Shew to me
the secret of woman, O Beauty, and enlighten me, for you are know-
ledge'. He said: 'She is you, human heart, and as you were, so was she.
She is I, and wheresoever I be, there is she. She is as a religion when the
ignorant profane it not; as a full moon when clouds do not hide it; as the
breeze untouched by corruption and impurity'.

Then my heart drew near to Wisdom, the daughter of Love and Beauty, saying: 'Give me wisdom that I may carry it to humankind'. She answered: 'Say that happiness begins in the holy of holies of the spirit and comes not from without'.

Translated by H M Nahmad

My birthday

(Written while studying art in Paris, 6th January 1908)

On the day my mother gave me birth,
On that day five-and-twenty years ago,
Silence placed me in the vast hands of life, abounding with
    struggle and conflict.
Lo, five-and-twenty times have I journeyed round the sun.
How many times the moon has journeyed round me I do not
    know.
But this I know, that I have not yet learned the secrets of light,
Nor have I understood the mysteries of darkness.

Five-and-twenty times have I journeyed with the earth, the
    moon, the sun and stars encircling the universe.
Lo, now my soul whispers the names of cosmic systems
Even as the caverns of the sea resound to the waves,
For the soul exists, a current in the cosmos, but does not know
    its power.
And the soul chants the cosmic rhythm, high and low,
Yet attains not the fullness of its harmonies.

Five-and-twenty years ago Time wrote me down in the book
    of this strange and awful life.
Lo, a word am I, signifying now nothing and now many
    things.
On that day of every year what thoughts and what memories
    throng my soul!
They halt before me – the procession of the days gone by,
The parade of the phantoms of the night –

Then are they swept away, even as the wind sweeps clouds
from the horizon;
They vanish in the darkness of my house as the songs of the
rivulets in desolate and distant valleys.

On that day, every year, those spirits which have shaped my
spirit
Come seeking me from the far ends of the worlds,
And chanting words of sorrowful remembrance.
Then they are gone, to hide behind the semblance of this life,
Even as birds descending to a threshing-floor and finding no
seeds to feast upon,
Hover but a moment and fly hence to seek another place.

Ever upon that day the meanings of my past life stand before
me, like dim mirrors
Wherein I look for a while and see naught but the pallid
corpse-like faces of the years,
Naught but the wrinkled and aged visages of hopes and
dreams long lost.

Once more I look upon those mirrors and there behold only
my own still face.
I gaze thereon beholding naught but sadness.
I question sadness and I find it has no speech;
Yet could sadness speak, methinks it would utter a sweeter
word than joy.

For five-and-twenty years I have loved much,
And oftentimes have I loved what others hate.
Yet what I loved as a child I love now,
And what I now love I shall love unto the end of life;
For love is all I have, and none shall make me lose it.

Oftentimes I have loved death,
Called death sweet names and spoken of it in loving words
both openly and secretly.
Yet though I have not forgotten, nor broken the vows of death,
I have learned to love life also.

For death and life have become equal to me in beauty and in joy;
They have shared in the growth of my yearning and desire,
And they have divided my love and tenderness.

Freedom also I have loved, even as life and death.
And as my love grew, so grew also my knowledge of men's slavery to tyranny and contempt,
The while I beheld their submission to idols hewn by the dark ages,
Reared in ignorance and polished by the lips of slaves.
But I loved these slaves as I loved freedom, and I pitied them, for they are blind men
Kissing the jaws of foul bloodthirsty beasts, and seeing not;
Sucking the venom of malignant vipers, and feeling not;
Digging their graves with their own hands, and knowing not.
Freedom have I loved more than aught else,
For I have found freedom like unto a maiden wasted from privation and seclusion
Till she became a ghost that moves among the houses in the lonely streets,
And when she calls out to the passers-by, they neither hear nor look.

Like all men, during these five-and-twenty years I have loved happiness;
I have learned to awake at every dawn and seek it, even as they.
But never have I found it in their ways.
Nor seen the trace of the footsteps of happiness on the sand near their mansions,
Nor have I heard the echo of its voice from the windows of their temples.
I sought alone to find it.
I heard my soul whisper in my ear:
'Happiness is a maiden born and reared in the fastness of the heart;
She comes never from beyond its walls'.
Yet when I opened the portal of my heart to find happiness,

I saw therein her mirror and her bed and her garments but
herself I could not find.

Mankind have I loved. Ay, much have I loved men,
And men in my opinion are three:
The one who curses life, the one who blesses it and the one
who contemplates it.
The first I have loved for his misery, the second for his bene-
ficence, and the third for his wisdom.

Thus passed five-and-twenty years,
And thus my days and nights, pursuing each other down my life
As the leaves of trees scatter before the winds of autumn.
And today I pause remembering, even as a weary climber half
way to the summit,
And I look backward, and to right and left, but I see no
treasure anywhere
Which I may claim and say: 'This is mine own'.

Nor do I find in the seasons of my years any harvest
Save only sheets of fair white paper traced over with markings
of black ink,
And strange and fragmentary canvases filled in with lines and
colours, both harmonious and inharmonious.
In these have I shrouded and buried the loveliness and the
freedom that I have thought and dreamed,
Even as the ploughman who goes to the field to sow his seeds
in furrows
Returns to his house at eventide hoping and waiting.
But I, though I have sowed well the seeds of my heart,
Yet I have neither hoped nor waited.
And now that I have reached this season of my life,
The past seems hidden behind a mist of sighs and grief,
And the future revealed through the veil of the past.

I pause and gaze at life from my small window;
I behold the faces of men, and I hear their shouting rise into
the sky.
I heed their footsteps falling among the streets of houses,

And I perceive the communion of their spirits, the eagerness
   of their desires, the yearning of their hearts.
I pause and behold the children throwing dust upon each
   other with laughter and loud cries.
I behold boys with their faces upward lifted as though they
   were reading an ode to youth written upon the margins of a
   cloud
Lined with the gleaming radiance of the sun.
I behold young maidens swaying to and fro, like branches of a
   tree,
Smiling like flowers, and gazing at the youths from behind
   eyelids
Quivering with love and soft desire.
I behold the aged walking slowly, with their low-bent backs.
Leaning upon their staffs and gazing fixedly at the earth
As if their old dim eyes were searching in the dust for lost
   bright jewels.
I pause beside my window and I gaze at all these shapes and
   shadows
Moving and creeping silently about the city.

Then I look afar beyond the city to the wilderness,
And I behold all that is therein of dreadful beauty and of
   calling silence,
Its lofty mounds and little valleys, its springing trees and
   tremulous grasses,
Its flowers with perfume laden, and its whispering rivers,
Its wild birds singing, and all its humming wingèd life.

I gaze beyond the wilderness, and there, behold, the ocean –
With its deep wonders and mysterious secrets, its hid treasures;
There I behold all that is upon the face of the raging, rushing,
   foaming waters,
And the spray that rises and the vapours that descend.

I peer far beyond the ocean and behold the infinity of space,
The drifting worlds, the glimmering constellations, the suns
   and moons, the fixed and the shooting stars;

And I behold the evidence of forces forever attracting and repelling, the wars of elements, creating, changing, and withal held prisoned within a law of no beginning and no end.

These things I contemplate through my small window, and I forget my five-and-twenty years,
And all the centuries which have preceded them,
And all the ages that shall follow.
Then my life, with its revelations and its mysteries, seems to me like the sighing of a child
That trembles in the void of the eternal depths and heights.
Yet this atom, this self that I call *I*, makes ever a stirring and a clamour,
Lifting its wings toward the vast firmament,
Reaching its hands toward the four corners of the earth,
Its being poised upon the point of time which gave it conscious life.

Then from the holy of holies where this living spark abides, a voice arises crying:
'Peace be with you, life!
Peace be with you, awakening!
Peace be with you, realization!
Peace be with you, day, whose abundant light enfolds the darkness of earth!
Peace be with you, night, whose darkness reveals the light of heaven!
Peace be with you, seasons!
Peace be with you, spring, that renews the youth of the earth!
Peace be with you, summer, that enriches the glory of the sun!
Peace be with you, autumn, that bestows the fruits of labour and the harvest of toil!
Peace be with you, winter, that restores with tempests the wasted strength of nature!
Peace be with you, years, which disclose what the years have hidden!
Peace be with you, ages, which restore what the centuries have destroyed!

Peace be with you, time, which moves with us unto the perfect
   day!
Peace be with you, spirit, that guards with prudence the reins
   of life, hidden from us by the sun!
Peace be with you, heart, that you are moved to acclaim peace
The while you bathe in tears!
Peace be with you, lips, that you utter peace
The while you taste the bread of bitterness!'.

Translated by A Ghareeb

The hymn of man

I was,
And I am.
So shall I be to the end of Time,
For I am without end.

I have cleft the vast spaces of the Infinite, and taken flight in the
   world of fantasy, and drawn nigh to the circle of light on high.
Yet behold me a captive of Matter.
I have hearkened to the teachings of Confucius, and listened
   to the wisdom of Brahma, and sat beside the Buddha
   beneath the tree of knowledge.
Behold me now contending with ignorance and unbelieving.
I was upon Sinai when the Lord shewed Himself to Moses. By
   the Jordan I beheld the Nazarene's miracles. In Medina I
   heard the words of the Apostle of Arabia.
Behold me now a prisoner of doubt.
I have seen Babylon's strength and Egypt's glory and the
   greatness of Greece. My eyes cease not upon the smallness
   and poverty of their works.
I have sat with the witch of Endor and the priests of Assyria
   and the prophets of Palestine, and I cease not to chant the
   truth.
I have learned the wisdom that descended on India, and
   gained mastery over poetry that welled from the Arabian's
   heart, and hearkened to the music of people from the West.

Yet blind and see not; my ears are stopped and I do not hear.
I have borne the harshness of insatiable conquerors, and felt
the oppression of tyrants and the bondage of the powerful.
Yet am I strong to do battle with the days.
All this have I heard and seen, and I am yet a child. In truth
shall I hear and see the deeds of youth, and grow old and
attain perfection and return to God.

I was,
And I am.
So shall I be to the end of Time,
For I am without end.

Translated by H M Nahmad

In the city of the dead

It was but yesterday I escaped the tumult of the city
And went forth to walk in the silent fields;
And I came unto a lofty hill
Where nature had bestowed the gifts of her bountiful hand.
I ascended the hill and looked back upon the city.
And lo, the city appeared, with all its towers and temples,
To lie beneath a cloud of thick dark smoke that rose up from
its forges and its factories.

As I sat contemplating from afar the works of man,
It seemed that most of them are vain and futile.
And heartily I turned my mind away from all that the sons of
Adam have wrought,
And looked upon the fields, the seat of God's great glory.
And in their midst I beheld a graveyard with tombstones of
fair marble, and with cypress trees.

There, between the city of the living and the city of the dead,
I sat
And mused upon the endless struggle and the ceaseless turbu-
lence in life,

And the enveloping silence and vast dignity in death.

On the one side I beheld hope and despair, love and hate, riches and poverty, belief and unbelief;

And on the other, dust in dust which nature intermingles,

Fashioning therefrom its world of green and growing things that thrive in the deep silence of the night.

While thus I pondered, behold, a great crowd, marching slowly, caught my vision,

And I heard music filling the air with dreary tunes.

Before my eyes passed a procession of the great and the lowly of mankind,

Walking together in procession at the funeral of a man who had been rich and powerful,

The dead followed by the living.

And these wept and cried aloud, filling the day with their wailings and their lamentations,

Even unto the burial-place.

And here the priests offered up prayers and swung their censers,

And the pipers blew mournfully upon their pipes.

The orators stood forth with sounding words of eulogy,

And the poets, bemoaning with their studied verses,

Until all had come unto a weary end.

And then the crowd dispersed, revealing a proud tombstone which the stonecutters had vied in making,

And many wreaths of flowers, and garlands woven by deft and skilful fingers.

Then the procession returned toward the city, while I sat watching from afar and musing.

And now the sun was sinking toward the west, and the shadows of the rocks and trees began to lengthen and discard their raiment of light.

At that moment I looked, and lo, two men bearing upon their shoulders a coffin of plain wood;

And after them a woman came in ragged garments,

A babe at her breast, and at her feet a dog that looked now to
the woman, now to the wooden casket.
Only these, in the procession at the funeral of a man who had
been poor and humble –
The wife whose silent tears bespoke her sorrow,
A baby crying because his mother wept, and a faithful beast
who would follow also in his dumb grief.
And when these reached the place of graves,
They lowered the coffin down into a pit in the far corner, well
removed from the lofty marble tombs.
Then they turned back in silence and in desolation,
And the dog's eyes looked oftentimes toward the last
dwelling-place of his friend and master,
Until they had disappeared from sight behind the trees.

Thereupon I bent my eyes first upon the city of the living, and
said to myself:
'This is for the rich and powerful men';
Then I looked upon the city of the dead, saying:
'And this is for the rich and powerful men.'
And I cried aloud: 'Where, then, is the abiding-place of those
who are weak and poor, O Lord?'
This I said, and gazed up toward the heaven of clouds, glori-
ous with the golden rays of the great sun.
And I heard a voice within me saying: 'It is there!'.

Translated by A Ghareeb

The poet

A LINK BETWEEN this world and the one yet to come; spring of
sweet waters refreshing all thirsty souls; a tree on the banks of
beauty, weighed down with ripe fruits which all hungry hearts
long and yearn for with ardent desire; a nightingale flitting through
branches of words as it sings melodies that fill the heart with gentleness
and peace; a white cloud appearing at twilight that rises and swells, to
fill heaven's face, then pour rain on the flowers in life's fields; an angel
sent by the gods to teach men their knowledge divine; a bright lamp

no darkness can quench, and no bushel can hide, filled with rich oil by Astarte, the goddess of love, and lit by Apollo, the god of music himself.

Clothed in simplicity, nourished on mildness, he sits alone in the lap of nature, responsive to learn creation's wonders and mysteries, all she can teach, awake in the stillness of the night to wait for the spirit's descent. He is the husbandman sowing his heart's precious seeds in the fields of emotion, that mankind may feed upon rich crops. This is the poet whom men ignore in this life to revere him only when he leaves this world for his true sublime home. It is he who asks naught of men but the slightest of smiles, whose rising breath fills the horizon with beauty and life; yet, in return, men deny him both shelter and bread.

How long, O man, how long, O universe, will you raise lofty mansions for those who defile earth's face with blood, and spurn those who give you their own inner beauty, peace, joy? How long will you glorify murderers, tyrants who bowed the necks of their brothers and sisters with slavery's yoke, and forget the men who spend all the light of their eyes in the darkness of night to teach you the glory of day, preyed on by misery so that no pleasure eludes you? And you, O poets, who are the very essence of life, you have conquered the ages despite their cruel disdain; winning the laurels of glory plucked from vanity's thorns; and built in men's hearts your kingdom, a realm without end.

Translated by S B Bushrui

From 'sawt al-sha'ir'

You are my brother and I love you.
I love you at prayer in your mosque,
at worship in your temple,
at your devotions in your church;
For you and I are the sons of one
                    religion the Spirit ...

Translated by S B Bushrui

FROM *AL-MAWAKIB*
(THE PROCESSIONS)

1919

This world is but a winery,
   Its host and master Father Time,
Who caters only to those steep'd
   In dreams discordant, without rhyme.

For people drink and race as though
   They were the steeds of mad desire;
Thus some are blatant when they pray,
   And others frenzied to acquire.

Few on this earth who savor life,
   And are not bor'd by its free gifts;
Or divert not its streams to cups
   In which their fancy floats and drifts.

Should you then find a sober soul
   Amidst this state of revelry,
Marvel how a moon did find
   In this rain cloud a canopy.

* * *

No confusion in the forest
   From illusion or from wine,
For the clouds endow the brook
   With elixir superfine.

Yet the human turns to drugging,
    As to nursing from the breast;
Coming to the age of weaning
    Only when he's put to rest.

Give to me the reed and sing thou!
    For the song is gracious shade,
And the plaint of reed remaineth
    When illusions dim and fade.

*   *   *

There is not a death in nature,
    Nor a grave is set apart;
Should the month of April vanish
    'Gifts of joy' do not depart.

Fear of death is a delusion
    Harbored in the breast of sages;
He who lives a single Springtime
    Is like one who lives for ages.

Give to me the reed and sing thou!
    For song is Immortality,
And the plaint of reed remaineth
    After the joy and misery.

*   *   *

Give to me the reed and sing thou!
    Forget hence what both have stated;
Words are but the motes in rainbow,
    Tell me now of joys you've tasted.

Have you taken to the forest,
    Shunned the palace for an abode?
Followed brooks in their courses,
    Climbed the rocks along the road?

Have you ever bathed in fragrance,
    Dried yourself in sheets of light?
Ever quaff the wine of dawning,
    From ethereal goblets bright?

Have you rested at the sunset,
　　As I have beneath the vine?
Laden with suspended clusters,
　　Ripened to golden crystalline?

Ever bedded in the herbage,
　　Quilted by a heavenly vast,
Unconcerned about the future,
　　And forgetful of your past?

Felt that the nocturnal silence,
　　Sea-like surged around your head,
That the breast of night had harbored
　　A throbbing heart within your bed?

Give to me the reed and sing thou!
　　Forget all the cures and ills,
Mankind is like verses written
　　Upon the surface of the rills.

What good is there, pray thee tell me,
　　In jostling through the crowd in life,
'Mid the argumental tumult,
　　Protestation, and endless strife;

Mole-like burrowing in darkness,
　　Grasping for the spider's thread,
Always thwarted in ambition,
　　Until the living join the dead?

*　*　*

Had I the days in hand to string,
　　Only in forest they'd be strewn,
But circumstances drive us on
　　In narrow paths by Kismet hewn.

For Fate has ways we cannot change,
　　While weakness preys upon our Will;
We bolster with excuse the self,
　　And help that Fate ourselves to kill.

Translated by G Kheirallah

FROM *AL-'AWASIF* (THE TEMPESTS)

1920

From 'Dead are my people' (written in exile during the famine in Syria)

World War I

... My people died from hunger, and he who
Did not perish from starvation was
Butchered with the sword; and I am
Here in this distant land, roaming
Amongst a joyful people who sleep
Upon soft beds, and smile at the days
While the days smile upon them.

My people died a painful and shameful
Death, and here am I living in plenty
And in peace .... This is deep tragedy
Ever-enacted upon the stage of my
Heart; few would care to witness this
Drama, for my people are as birds with
Broken wings, left behind by the flock ....

I am here beyond the
Broad seas living in the shadow of
Tranquility, and in the sunshine of
Peace .... I am afar from the pitiful
Arena and the distressed, and cannot
Be proud of aught, not even of my own
Tears.

What can an exiled son do for his
Starving people, and of what value
Unto them is the lamentation of an
Absent poet? ...

And oftentime they say unto me,
'The disaster of your country is
But naught to the calamity of the
World, and the tears and blood shed
By your people are as nothing to
The rivers of blood and tears
Pouring each day and night in the
Valleys and plains of the earth ....'

... If my nation had partaken in the war
Of all nations and had died in the
Field of battle, I would say that
The raging tempest had broken with
Its might the green branches; and
Strong death under the canopy of
The tempest is nobler than slow
Perishing in the arms of senility.
But there was no rescue from the
Closing jaws .... My people dropped
And wept with the crying angels.

If an earthquake had torn my
Country asunder and the earth had
Engulfed my people into its bosom,
I would have said, 'A great and
Mysterious law has been moved by

The will of divine force, and it
Would be pure madness if we frail
Mortals endeavoured to probe its
Deep secrets ...'.

But my people did not die as rebels;
They were not killed in the field
Of battle; nor did the earthquake
Shatter my country and subdue them.
Death was their only rescuer, and
Starvation their only spoils.

My people died on the cross ....
They died while their hands
Stretched toward the East and West,
While the remnants of their eyes
Stared at the blackness of the
Firmament .... They died silently,
For humanity had closed its ears
To their cry. They died because
They did not befriend their enemy.
They died because they loved their
Neighbours. They died because
They placed trust in all humanity.
They died because they did not
Oppress the oppressors. They died
Because they were the crushed
Flowers, and not the crushing feet.
They died because they were peace
Makers. They perished from hunger
In a land rich with milk and honey.
They died because the monsters of
Hell arose and destroyed all that
Their fields grew, and devoured the
Last provisions in their bins ....
They died because the vipers and
Sons of vipers spat out poison into
The space where the Holy Cedars and

The roses and the jasmine breathe
Their fragrance ....

Translated by A R Ferris

At the door of the temple

I purified my lips with the sacred fire to speak of love,
But when I opened my lips I found myself speechless.
Before I knew love, I was wont to chant the songs of love,
But when I learned to know, the words in my mouth became
    naught save breath,
And the tunes within my breast fell into deep silence.
In the past, when you would question me concerning the
    secrets and the mysteries of love,
I would speak and answer you with assurance.
But now that love has adorned me with vestments,
I come, in my turn, to question you of all the ways of love, and
    all its wonders.
Who among you can answer me?
I come to question you about my self and that which is in me.
Who among you can reveal my heart to my heart,
And disclose myself to my self?
Tell me now, what flame is this that burns within my bosom,
Consuming my strength, and melting my hopes and my desires?
What hands are these, light, gentle, and alluring,
Which enfold my spirit in its hours of loneliness
And pour into the vessel of my heart a wine mixed of the bit-
    terness of joy
And the sweetness of pain?
What wings are these beating around my bed in the long
    silence of the night,
So that I am wakeful, watching – I know not what;
Listening to that I do not hear, and gazing upon that I do not
    see;
Meditating on that I do not comprehend, and possessing that
    I have not attained.

Ay, wakeful am I, sighing,

For to me sighs and griefs are lovelier than the ring of joy and laughter;

Wakeful am I in the hand of an unseen power that slays me and then quickens me,

Even until the day dawns and fills the corners of my house with light.

Then do I sleep, while between my withered eyelids the shadows of my wakefulness still quiver,

And above my bed of stone hovers the figure of a dream.

* * *

And what is this that we call love?

Tell me, what is this mystic secret hiding behind the semblance of our life,

And living in the heart of our existence?

What is this vast release coming as a cause to all effects, and as an effect unto all causes?

What is this quickening that gathers death and life and from them creates a dream

More strange than life, and deeper far than death?

Tell me, my brothers, tell me, which of you would not awake from this sleep of life

When your spirit feels the touch of love's white fingers?

Which of you would not forsake his father and his mother and his birthplace

When the maiden his heart loves calls out to him?

Which of you would not cross the desert and climb the mountain and sail the seas

To seek her to whom your spirit yearns?

What youth, indeed, would not follow to the earth's uttermost bounds,

If one awaits him there whose breath and voice and touch he shall find sweet and wholesome?

What man would not thus burn his soul as incense

Before a god who regards his craving and grants him his petition?

* * *

It was but yesterday that I stood at the door of the temple
Questioning the passers-by concerning the mysteries and the
    benefits of love.
And a man passed by, of middle age, wasted and with a scowl-
    ing countenance, and he said:
'Love is an inborn weakness which we have inherited from the
    first man'.
Then a youth, strong and stalwart of body and arm, came
    chanting:
'Love is a resolution which accompanies our being, and binds
    this present with the ages past and future'.
And now a sad-faced woman, passing, sighed and said:
'Love is a deadly venom which dark and fearful vipers diffuse
    in space from the abyss of hell,
So that it descends in dew upon the thirsty soul,
And the soul therefrom becomes for a moment drunken, then
    sobered for a year, and dead an æon'.
But a young maiden, rosy, and with laughing lips, said:
'See, love is a nectar which the brides of dawn pour for the strong
So that they rise glorified before the stars of night, and joyous
    before the sun of day'.
Thereafter came a man in a garment of sombre black and a
    loose beard that fell upon his breast, and he said sternly:
'Love is a stupidity which comes with the dawn of youth and is
    gone with its eventide'.
And one followed him with face radiant and serene, saying in
    tranquil joy:
'Love is a heavenly wisdom that lights our inner and outer eye
So that we may behold all things even as the gods'.
Then passed by a blind man questioning the ground with his
    old staff, and there was a wailing in his voice as he said:
'Love is a dense fog to enshroud the soul, and veil from it the
    shows of life,
So that the soul sees naught but the shadows of its desires
Lost among rocky steeps,
And hears naught but the echo of its voice shouting from the
    valleys of desolation'.

Then passed by a young man playing upon a lyre and singing:
'Love is a celestial light shining from the innermost of the sensitive self to illumine all about it,
That it may behold the worlds as a procession moving in green meadows,
And life as a dream of beauty between awakening and awakening'.
And after the young man followed one decrepit, and with dragging feet, trembling, and he said:
'Love is the repose of the sad body in the silent grave,
And it is the security of the soul in the fastnesses of eternity'.
Then came a young child whose years were but five, and he ran and shouted:
'Love is my father, and love is my mother,
And no one knows of love but my mother and my father'.

* * *

And now the day was done and all the people were passed by before the temple,
And each and every one had spoken of love,
And in each word he had revealed his own longing and desire
And had disclosed the secret mysteries of life.

When evening was fully come, and the moving throng had gone their ways,
And all was hushed,
I heard a voice within the temple saying:
'All life is twain, the one a frozen stream, the other a burning flame,
And the burning flame is love'.

Thereupon I entered into the temple and bowed myself, kneeling in supplication
And chanting a prayer in my secret heart:
'Make me, O Lord, food for the burning flame,
And make me, O God, fuel for the sacred fire.
Amen'.

Translated by A Ghareeb

Revelation

When the night waxed deep and slumber cast its cloak upon
    the face of the earth,
I left my bed and sought the sea, saying to myself:
'The sea never sleeps, and the wakefulness of the sea brings
    comfort to a sleepless soul'.
When I reached the shore, the mist had already descended
    from the mountain tops
And covered the world as a veil adorns the face of a maiden.

There I stood gazing at the waves, listening to their singing,
    and considering the power that lies behind them –
The power that travels with the storm, and rages with the vol-
    cano, that smiles with smiling flowers and makes melody
    with murmuring brooks.

After a while I turned, and lo,
I beheld three figures sitting upon a rock near by,
And I saw that the mist veiled them, and yet it veiled them not.

Slowly I walked toward the rock whereon they sat, drawn by
    some power which I know not.
A few paces off I stood and gazed upon them, for there was
    magic in the place
Which crystallized my purpose and bestirred my fancy.
And at that moment one of the three arose, and with a voice
    that seemed to come from the sea depths he said:
'Life without love is like a tree without blossoms or fruit.
And love without beauty is like flowers without fragrance, and
    fruit without seeds.
Life, Love, and Beauty are three entities in one self, free and
    boundless,
Which know neither change nor separation'.
This he said, and sat again in his place.

Then the second figure arose, and with a voice like the roar of
    rushing waters he said:
'Life without rebellion is like the seasons without a spring.

And rebellion without right is like spring in an arid and barren
  desert.
Life, Rebellion, and Right are three entities in one self,
And in them is neither change nor separation'.
This he said, and sat again in his place.

Then the third figure arose, and spoke with a voice like the
  peal of thunder, saying:
'Life without freedom is like a body without a spirit.
And freedom without thought is like a spirit confounded.
Life, Freedom, and Thought are three entities in one eternal self,
Which neither vanish nor pass away'.

Then the three arose and with voices of majesty and awe they
  spoke:
'Love and all that it begets,
Rebellion and all that it creates,
Freedom and all that it generates,
These three are aspects of God ...
And God is the infinite mind of the finite and conscious world'.

Then silence followed, filled with the stirring of invisible
  wings and the tremor of ethereal bodies.
And I closed my eyes, listening to the echo of the saying which
  I heard.

When I opened my eyes, I beheld naught but the sea hidden
  beneath a blanket of mist;
And I moved closer toward that rock
And I beheld naught but a pillar of incense rising unto the sky.

Translated by A Ghareeb

Night

O Night, abiding-place of poets and of lovers and of singers,
O Night, where shadows dwell with spirits and with visions,
O Night, enfolder of our longing, our desire, our memory,
Vast giant standing betwixt the dwarfed evening clouds and
  the brides of dawn,

Girt with the sword of awe, crowned with the moon, and garmented with silence;
Who gazes with a thousand eyes into the depths of life,
And listens with a thousand ears to the sighs of desolation and of death!

* * *

It is your darkness that reveals to us the light of heaven,
For the light of day has enshrouded us with the darkness of earth.
It is your promise that opens our eyes to eternity,
For the vanity of day had held us like blind men in the world of time and space.
It is your tranquil silence that unveils the secret of ever wakeful, ever restless spirits;
For day is a turbulent clamour wherein souls lie beneath the sharp hooves of ambition and desire.
O Night, you are a shepherd who gathers unto the fold of sleep the dreams of the weak and the hopes of the strong.
You are a seer who closes with his mystic fingers the eyelids of the wretched and lifts their hearts to a world more kindly than this world.
In the folds of your grey garments lovers have found their bower,
And upon your feet, wet with the dew of heaven, have the lonely-hearted wept their tears;
In the palms of your hands, fragrant with the scent of field and vineyard, strangers have laid down their longing and despair;
To lovers you are a friend; to the lonely, a comforter; to the desolate, a host.
In your deep shade the poet's fancies stir; on your bosom the prophetic heart awakes; upon your brow imagination writes.
For to the poet you are a sovereign, to the prophet a vision and to the thinker an intimate.

* * *

When my soul became weary of man, and my eyes were tired of gazing upon the face of the day,

I sought the distant fields where the shadows of bygone ages sleep.

There I stood before a dark and silent being moving with a thousand feet over the mountain, and over the valley and the plain.

There I gazed into the eyes of darkness and listened to the murmuring of invisible wings.

There I felt the touch of formless garments and was shaken by the terrors of the unseen.

There I saw you, Night, tragic and beautiful and awesome,

Standing between the heaven and the earth, with clouds for your garment, girdled with the fog,

Laughing at the light of the sun and mocking the supremacy of the day,

Deriding the multitude of slaves who kneel sleepless before their idols and contemptuous of kings who lie asleep and dreaming in their beds of silk,

There I beheld you gazing into the eyes of thieves and I beheld you keeping guard above the babe in slumber;

I saw you weeping before the smiles of prostitutes and smiling at the tears of lovers,

And lifting with your right hand the great-hearted and with your feet trampling the mean-spirited.

There I saw you, Night, and you saw me;

You, in your awful beauty, were to me a father and I, in my dreams, was a son;

For the curtains of being were drawn away and the veil of doubt was rent;

You revealed your secret purposes unto me and I told you all my hopes and my desires.

Then was your majesty turned into melody more beautiful than the gentle whisper of flowers,

And my fears were transformed into trust more than the trust of birds;

And you lifted me and placed me on your shoulders,

And you taught my eyes to see, my ears to hear, my lips to speak, and my heart to love;

With your magic fingers you touched my thought,
And my thought poured forth like a flowing, singing stream,
  bearing away all that was withered grass.
And with your lips you kissed my spirit and it kindled into flames
Devouring every dead and dying thing.

* * *

I followed you, O Night, until I became like unto you;
I went as your companion until your desires became mine;
I loved you until my whole being was indeed a lesser image of
  your own.
For within my dark self are glowing stars which passion scat-
  ters at evening and doubt gathers at dawn;
And within my heart is a moon that struggles, now with thick
  clouds, and now with a procession of dreams that fills all space.
Now within my awakened soul dwells a peace that reveals the
  lover's secret and the worshipper's prayer;
And upon my head rests a veil of mystery which the agony of
  death may rend, but the songs of youth shall weave again.

I am like you, O Night, and if men shall deem me boastful,
Do they not boast of their resemblance to the day?
I am like you, and like you I am accused of much that I am not.
I am like you with all my dreams and all my hopes and being.
I am like you, even though dusk does not crown me with its
  golden fleece.
I am like you, though morn does not adorn my trailing raiment
  with pearl and rose.
I am like you, though I am not yet belted with the Milky Way.
I too am a night, vast and calm, yet fettered and rebellious.
There is no beginning to my darkness and no end to my depths.
When the souls of the departed rise to pride themselves upon
  the light of joy,
My night soul shall descend glorified by the darkness of its sorrow.
I am like you, O Night, and when my dawn comes, then also
  shall come my end.

Translated by A Ghareeb

FROM *AL-BADAYI' WA AL-TARAY'IF* (BEAUTIFUL AND RARE SAYINGS)

1923

My soul counselled me

My soul spoke unto me and counselled me to love all that
  others hate,
And to befriend those whom others defame.
My soul counselled me and revealed unto me that love
  dignifies not alone the one who loves, but also the beloved.
Unto that day love was for me a thread of cobweb between two
  flowers, close to one another;
But now it has become a halo with neither beginning nor end,
Encircling all that has been and waxing eternally to embrace
  all that shall be.

* * *

My soul counselled me and taught me to see beauty veiled by
  form and colour.
My soul charged me to gaze steadfastly upon all that is deemed
  ugly until it appears lovely.

Before my soul had thus charged and counselled me,
I had seemed to see beauty like unto wavering torches between
pillars of smoke;
But now the smoke has dispersed and vanished and I see
naught but the burning.

*   *   *

My soul counselled me and charged me to listen for voices that
rise neither from the tongue nor the throat.
Before that day I heard but dully, and naught save clamour and
loud cries came to my ears;
But now I have learned to listen to silence,
To hear its choirs singing the songs of ages,
Chanting the hymns of space, and disclosing the secrets of
eternity.

*   *   *

My soul spoke unto me and counselled me to quench my thirst
with that wine which may not be poured into cups,
Nor lifted by hands, nor touched by lips.
Unto that day my thirst was like a dim spark laid in ashes
To be put out by a draught from any spring;
But now my strong yearning has become my cup,
Love has become my wine, and loneliness my joy.

*   *   *

My soul counselled me and charged me to seek that which is
unseen;
And my soul revealed unto me that the thing we grasp is the
thing we desire.
In other days I was content with warmth in winter, and with a
cooling zephyr in the summer season;
But now my fingers are become as mist,
Letting fall all that they have held, to mingle with the unseen
that I now desire.

*   *   *

My soul spoke to me and invited me to breathe the fragrance
   from a plant
That has neither root nor stalk nor blossom, and that no eye
   has seen.
Before my soul counselled me thus, I sought perfumes in the
   gardens,
In jars of sweet-smelling herbs and vessels of incense;
But now I am aware only of an incense that may not be burned,
I breathe an air more fragrant than all earth's gardens and all
   the winds of space.

* * *

My soul counselled me and charged me to answer and say: 'I
   follow,' when the unknown and the adventurous call unto
   me.
Hitherto I had answered naught but the voice of the crier in
   the market-place,
Nor did I pursue aught save roads charted and well
   trodden;
But now the known has become a steed that I mount to seek
   the unknown,
And the road has become a ladder by which I may climb to the
   perilous summit.
My soul counselled me and admonished me to measure time
   with this saying:
'There was a yesterday and there shall be a tomorrow'.
Unto that hour I deemed the past an epoch that is lost and
   shall be forgotten,
And the future I deemed an era that I may not attain;
But now I have learned this:
That in the brief present all time, with all that is in time,
Is achieved and come true.

* * *

My soul spoke and revealed unto me that I am not bound in
   space by the words:
'Here, there, and over there'.

Hitherto I stood upon my hill, and every other hill seemed
    distant and far away;
But now I know that the hill whereon I dwell is indeed all hills,
And the valley whereunto I descend comprehends all valleys.
My soul counselled me and besought me to watch while
    others sleep
And to seek my pillow while they are wakeful,
For in all my years I had not perceived their dreams, nor they
    mine.
But now I am winged by day in my dreaming,
And when they sleep I behold them free upon the night,
And I rejoice in their freedom.

* * *

My soul counselled me and charged me lest I be exalted
    because of over-praise
And lest I be distressed for fear of blame.
Until that day I doubted the worth of my own handiwork;
But now I have learned this:
That the trees blossom in spring, and bear fruit in summer,
And drop their leaves in autumn to become utterly naked in
    winter
Without exaltation and without fear or shame.
My soul counselled me and assured me
That I am neither higher than the pygmy nor lower than the
    giant.
Before that day I beheld mankind as two men,
The one a weakling whom I derided or pitied,
And the other a mighty man whom I would either follow, or
    oppose in rebellion.
But now I know that I was formed even from the same dust of
    which all men are created,
That my elements are their elements, and my inner self is their
    inner self.
My struggle is their struggle, and their pilgrimage is mine
    own.
If they transgress, I am also the transgressor,

And if they do well, then I have a share in their well-doing.
If they arise, I too arise with them; if they stay behind, I also,
    to company them.

* * *

My soul counselled me and instructed me to see that the light
    which I carry is not my light,
That my song was not created within me;
For though I travel with the light, I am not the light,
And though I am a lute fastened with strings,
I am not the lute-player.

* * *

My soul counselled me, my brother and enlightened me.
And oftentimes has your counselled and enlightened you.
For you are like me, and there is no difference between us
Save that I speak of what is within me in words that I have
    heard in my silence,
And you guard what is within you, and your guardianship is as
    goodly as my much speaking.

Translated by A Ghareeb

Be still, my heart

Be still, my heart. Space does not hear you.
Be still, my heart. The ether, heavy with mourning and with
    lamentation, will not bear your songs.
Be still, for the phantoms of night will not heed the whisper of
    your mysteries,
And the procession of darkness will not halt before your
    dreams.
Be still, my heart, be still until dawn.
For whose waits the morning patiently will greet the morning
    with strength,
And whoso loves the light, by light shall be loved.
Be still, my heart, and listen to my words.

In dreams I heard a blackbird singing above the mouth of a raging volcano,
And saw a lily lifting its head above the snow;
I saw a naked houri dancing among tombstones,
And a babe laughing the while it played with skulls.
All this I saw in a dream.

When I waked and looked about me, lo, I saw the volcano pouring forth its fury,
But I could not hear the blackbird singing.
I saw the heavens scattering snow over the hills and valleys,
Garmenting with its white shroud the silent lilies.
I saw the graves, row upon row, standing before the tranquillity of ages, but none amongst them dancing or praying.

Then I beheld hills of skulls, but no laughter was there save the laughing wind.
Waking I saw naught but grief and sorrow.
Where, then, have the joys of dreams departed?
Where hides the splendour of our sleep,
And how has its image vanished?
How can the soul bear patiently until the shadow of its yearning shall return with sleep?

*   *   *

Be still, my heart, and attend unto my words.
It was but yesterday that my soul was a tree, old and strong,
Whose roots penetrated to the depths of the earth and whose branches reached toward the infinite, blooming in spring and bearing fruit in summer.
When autumn was come, I gathered the fruit on trays of silver and placed them at the cross-roads,
And the passers-by reached for the fruit and ate of it and walked their way.

When autumn was passed and its song was turned to wailing and a dirge,
I looked upon my trays and saw that men had left there but a single fruit;

And when I tasted, I found it bitter as aloes and sour as a green
  grape.
Then I said to myself:
'Woe unto me, for I have placed a curse upon the lips of men,
  and hostility in their bowels.
What then, my soul, have you done with the sweetness that
  your roots had sucked from the bosom of earth,
And with fragrance that your boughs had drunk from the light
  of the sun'?

Thereupon I uprooted the old and strong tree of my soul.
I severed it from its past and dismantled it of the memories of
  a thousand springs and a thousand autumns.

And I planted the tree of my soul in another place.
I set it in a field far from the roads of time, and I passed the
  night in wakefulness beside it, giving it to drink of my tears
  and my blood, and saying:
'There is a savour in blood, and a sweetness in tears'.

When spring returned, the tree of my soul bloomed again, and
  bore fruit in the summer season.
And when the autumn was come, I gathered the ripe fruit once
  more, and I placed it upon trays of gold at the meeting-
  place of the roads.
And men passed by, but no one reached to take of the fruit.
Then I took and ate, and I found the fruit as sweet as honey, as
  luscious as nectar, perfumed as the breath of jasmine, and
  mellow as the wine of Babylon.
And I cried aloud, saying:
'Men do not desire blessedness upon their lips, nor truth in
  their bowels;
For blessedness is the daughter of tears, and truth is but the
  son of pain'.
Then I returned and sat down under the shade of the
  lonely tree of my soul, and in the field far from the roads of
  time.

* * *

Be still, my heart, be still until dawn.

Be still, for space is heavy with the odour of dead things and cannot inhale your living breath.

Be still, my heart, and listen to my voice.

It was but yesterday that my thought was like a ship, rocked upon the waves of the sea, and moving with the winds from shore to shore.

And the ship of my thought was empty save only for seven phials filled to the brim with seven colours, even the seven colours of the rainbow.

There came a time when I grew weary of drifting upon the face of the waters, and I said:

'I will return with the empty ship of my thought to the harbour of the town where I was born'.

And as I sailed, I began to paint the sides of my ship with the seven colours;

And it shone yellow as the sunset, azure like the sky, and red as a blood-red anemone;

And upon its sails and rudder I traced sketches to allure and delight the eye.

And when it was done, the ship of my thought appeared like the vision of a prophet

Floating betwixt the two infinities, the sea and the sky.

Now, when my ship reached port, behold, all the people came to meet me;

With shout and joy they welcomed me and they took me into the city,

Beating their tambourines and blowing upon their reed flutes.

All this they did because my ship appeared enchanting to their eyes;

But none boarded the ship of my thought,

Nor did any perceive that I had brought my ship empty into port.

Then I said to myself:

'I have misled the people, and with seven phials of colours have I deceived their inner and their outer eye'.

And when a year passed, again I boarded the ship of my thought and put out to sea.

I sailed to the isles of the East, and there I gathered myrrh and frankincense and sandalwood and brought them to my ship.

I sailed to the isles of the South, and from thence I brought gold, jade, and emerald, and every precious stone;

To the isles of the North I sailed, and found rare silks and velvets and broideries of every kind;

Thence to the isles of the West and got me coats of mail, and spears and swords, and divers weapons.

Thus I filled the ship of my thought with the costly and strange things of the earth,

And I turned back to the harbour of my own city, saying in my heart:

'Now shall my people praise me as a man worthy of praise.

And now shall they indeed lead me into the market-place with singing and piping'.

But, behold, when I reached the port, no man came to meet and welcome me.

Alone I entered the streets of my city, but no man looked upon me.

Even in the market-squares I stood, telling of all that I had brought of the earth's fruit and goodly things.

But the people looked upon me with laughter on their faces, and derision on their lips.

And they turned from me.

Thus was I troubled and cast down, and I turned me to the harbour.

No sooner did my eyes fall upon my ship than I became aware of a certain thing to which, in my voyaging and seeking for good cargoes, I had paid no heed;

So I cried out in humiliation:

'Behold, the waves of the sea have washed the seven colours from my ship

And now it appears but as a skeleton of bones.

And the winds and the storms and the heat of the sun have
    effaced from the sails the images of wonder and delight,
And they seem now but as a faded and tattered garment.
Truly I have gathered the earth's costly treasures in a casket
    floating upon the surface of the waters,
And returned unto my people, but they turn from me,
For their eyes see naught but outward show'.

At that very moment I abandoned the ship of my thought and
    sought the city of the dead,
Where I sat amid the whitened graves and pondered their secrets.
Be still, my heart. Be still until dawn.
Be still, though the tempest mock the whispering of your depths.
Be still, my heart, until dawn,
For whoso awaits the morning patiently,
The morning shall embrace him tenderly.

Behold, my heart, the dawn is come;
Speak, then, if you have yet the power of words.
Behold, my heart, the procession of the morning.
Did not the silence of the night stir in your depths a song with
    which to greet the morn?

Behold, the flight of doves and blackbirds above the valley;
Did not the awe of night strengthen your wings to fly with them?
Behold, the shepherds leading their flocks from the folds.
Did not the shadows of night urge your desire to follow also
    into the green meadows?
Behold, the young men and the maidens hastening toward the
    vineyard.
Would you not rise and join them?

Arise, my heart. Arise and move with the dawn.
For night is passed and the fears of night have vanished with
    their black dreams.
Arise, my heart, and lift your voice in song;
For he who joins not the dawn with this singing is but a child
    of darkness.

Translated by A Ghareeb

Fame

I walked upon the sand at ebb-tide.
And bending down, I wrote a line upon the sand.
And in that line I wrote what my mind thought
And what my soul desired.

And when the tide was high,
I returned to that very shore,
And of that which I had written I found naught.
I found only the staff-marks of one who had walked blindly.

Translated by A Ghareeb

Earth

With might and power earth springs forth out of earth;
Then earth moves over earth with dignity and pride;
And earth from earth builds palaces for kings,
And lofty towers and goodly temples for all people,
And weaves strange myths, strict laws and subtle dogmas.

When all these things are done, earth wearies of earth's
    labour,
And from its light and darkness it creates grey shadows and
    soft drowsy fancies and enchanting dreams.
Earth's slumber then beguiles earth's heavy eyelids,
And they close upon all things in deep and quiet slumber.

And earth calls out unto earth, saying:
'Behold, a womb am I and I am a tomb;
A womb and a tomb I shall remain forever,
Ay, even until the stars are no more,
And until the suns are turned into dead ashes'.

Translated by A Ghareeb

From 'Iram, city of lofty pillars'

TIME AND place are spiritual states and all that is seen and heard is spiritual. If you close your eyes you will perceive all things through the depths of your inner self and you will see the world physical and ethereal, in its intended entirety and you will acquaint yourself with its necessary laws and precautions and you will understand the greatness that it possesses beyond its closeness. Yes ... if you will close your eyes and open your heart and your inner perception you will discover the beginning and the end of existence ... that beginning which in its turn becomes an ending and that ending which must surely become a beginning ...

All things in this creation exist within you and all things in you exist in creation; there is no border between you and the closest things and there is no distance between you and the farthest things and all things, from the lowest to the loftiest, from the smallest to the greatest, are within you as equal things. In one atom are found all the elements of the earth; in one motion of the mind are found the motions of all the laws of existence; in one drop of water are found the secrets of all the endless oceans; in one aspect of *you* are found all the aspects of *existence*.

Translated by A R Ferris

Yesterday, today and tomorrow

I said to my friend,
  'See her leaning over his arm?
  Yesterday she leaned over my arm'.
And he said:
  'Tomorrow she will lean over mine'.
And I said:
  'See her sitting at his side;
  And yesterday she sat at my side'.
And he said:
  'Tomorrow she will sit at mine'.
And I said,
  'Don't you see her drinking from his cup?

And yesterday she sipped from mine'.
And he said:
'Tomorrow she will drink from mine'.
And I said,
'Look how she glances at him with eyes full of love!
And with just such love, yesterday she glanced at me'.
And he said:
'Tomorrow she will glance at me likewise'.
And I said,
'Listen to her whispering songs of love in his ears.
And yesterday she whispered the same songs in mine'.
And he said:
'Tomorrow she will whisper them in mine'.
And I said,
'Look at her embracing him; and yesterday she embraced
me'.
And he said:
'Tomorrow she will lie in my arms'.
And I said,
'What a strange woman she is!!'
And he said:
'She is Life'.

Translated by A R Ferris

The thrush

Sing, O thrush, song is the mystery of being.
Would I were, like you, free from cages and chains.
Would I were, like you, a spirit flying through the valley's open
    spaces
Drinking light as wine in cups of ether.
Would I were as pure as you, satisfied and contented,
Heedless of what is to come, and unaware of what has passed.
Would I were, like you, gentle beautiful and glorious;
My wings spread wide by the wind to be embroidered with the
    dew.

Would I were, like you, a thought floating over the hills,
Pouring forth my songs abroad, between forest and cloud.
Sing, O thrush, and dispel my sorrows;
In your voice there breathes a voice in my innermost ear.

Translated by S B Bushrui

SELECTIONS FROM GIBRAN'S ENGLISH WORKS

FROM *THE MADMAN*

1918

[*Thus I became madman*]

You ask me how I became a madman. It happened thus: One day, long before many gods were born, I woke from a deep sleep and found all my masks were stolen – the seven masks I have fashioned and worn in seven lives, – I ran maskless through the crowded streets shouting, 'Thieves, thieves, the curséd thieves'.

Men and women laughed at me and some ran to their houses in fear of me.

And when I reached the market place, a youth standing on a house-top cried, 'He is a madman'. I looked up to behold him; the sun kissed my own naked face for the first time. For the first time the sun kissed my own naked face and my soul was inflamed with love for the sun, and I wanted my masks no more. And as if in a trance I cried, 'Blessed, blessed are the thieves who stole my masks'.

Thus I became a madman.

And I have found both freedom and safety in my madness; the freedom of loneliness and the safety from being understood, for those who understand us enslave something in us.

But let me not be too proud of my safety. Even a Thief in jail is safe from another thief.

The grave-digger

ONCE, AS I was burying one of my dead selves, the gravedigger came by and said to me, 'Of all those who come here to bury, you alone I like'.

Said I, 'You please me exceedingly, but why do you like me'?

'Because', said he, 'They come weeping and go weeping – you only come laughing and go laughing'.

The good God and the evil God

The Good God and the Evil God met on the mountain top.

The Good God said, 'Good day to you, brother'.

The Evil God made no answer.

And the Good God said, 'You are in a bad humour today'.

'Yes', said the Evil God, 'for of late I have been often mistaken for you, called by your name, and treated as if I were you, and it ill-pleases me'.

And the Good God said, 'But I too have been mistaken for you and called by your name'.

The Evil God walked away cursing the stupidity of man.

'The perfect world'

God of lost souls, thou who art lost amongst the gods, hear me:

Gentle Destiny that watcheth over us, mad, wandering spirits, hear me:

I dwell in the midst of a perfect race, I the most imperfect.

I, a human chaos, a nebula of confused elements, I move amongst finished worlds – peoples of complete laws and pure order, whose thoughts are assorted, whose dreams are arranged, and whose visions are enrolled and registered.

Their virtues, O God, are measured, their sins are weighed, and even the countless things that pass in the dim twilight of neither sin nor virtue are recorded and catalogued.

Here days and nights are divided into seasons of conduct and governed by rules of blameless accuracy.

To eat, to drink, to sleep, to cover one's nudity, and then to be weary in due time.

To work, to play, to sing, to dance, and then to lie still when the clock strikes the hour.

To think thus, to feel thus much, and then to cease thinking and feeling when a certain star rises above yonder horizon.

To rob a neighbour with a smile, to bestow gifts with a graceful wave of the hand, to praise prudently, to blame cautiously, to destroy a soul with a word, to burn a body with a breath, and then to wash the hands when the day's work is done.

To love according to an established order, to entertain one's best self in a preconceived manner, to worship the gods becomingly, to intrigue the devils artfully – and then to forget all as though memory were dead.

To fancy with a motive, to contemplate with consideration, to be happy sweetly, to suffer nobly – and then to empty the cup so that tomorrow may fill it again.

All these things, O God, are conceived with forethought, born with determination, nursed with exactness, governed by rules, directed by reason, and then slain and buried after a prescribed method. And even their silent graves that lie within the human soul are marked and numbered.

It is a perfect world, a world of consummate excellence, a world of supreme wonders, the ripest fruit in God's garden, the master-thought of the universe.

But why should I be here, O God, I a green seed of unfulfilled passion, a mad tempest that seeketh neither east nor west, a bewildered fragment from a burnt planet?

Why am I here, O God of lost souls, thou who art lost amongst the gods?

FROM *THE FORERUNNER*

1920

[*You are your own forerunner*]

Y OU ARE your own forerunner, and the towers you have builded are but the foundation of your giant-self. And that self too shall be a foundation.

And I too am my own forerunner, for the long shadow stretching before me at sunrise shall gather under my feet at the noon hour. Yet another sunrise shall lay another shadow before me, and that also shall be gathered at another noon.

Always have we been our own forerunners, and always shall we be. And all that we have gathered and shall gather shall be but seeds for fields yet unploughed. We are the fields and the ploughmen, the gatherers and the gathered.

When you were a wandering desire in the mist, I too was there, a wandering desire. Then we sought one another and out of our eagerness dreams were born. And dreams were time limitless, and dreams were space without measure.

And when you were a silent word upon Life's quivering lips, I too was there, another silent word. Then Life uttered us and we came down the years throbbing with memories of yesterday and with longing for tomorrow, for yesterday was death conquered and tomorrow was birth pursued.

And now we are in God's hands. You are a sun in His right hand and I an earth in His left hand. Yet you are not more, shining, than I, shone upon.

And we, sun and earth, are but the beginning of a greater sun and a greater earth. And always shall we be the beginning.

*   *   *

You are your own forerunner, you the stranger passing by the gate of my garden.

And I too am my own forerunner, though I sit in the shadows of my trees and seem motionless.

The plutocrat

I N MY wanderings I once saw upon an island a man-headed, iron-hoofed monster who ate of the earth and drank of the sea incessantly. And for a long while I watched him. Then I approached him and said, 'Have you never enough; is your hunger never satisfied and your thirst never quenched?'

And he answered saying, 'Yes, I am satisfied, nay, I am weary of eating and drinking; but I am afraid that tomorrow there will be no more earth to eat and no more sea to drink'.

The weather-cock

S AID THE weather-cock to the wind, 'How tedious and monotonous you are! Can you not blow any other way but in my face? You disturb my God-given stability'.

And the wind did not answer. It only laughed in space.

Out of my deeper heart

Out of my deeper heart a bird rose and flew skyward.
Higher and higher did it rise, yet larger and larger did it grow.
At first it was like a swallow, then a lark, then an eagle, then as
vast as a spring cloud and then it filled the starry heavens.
Out of my heart a bird flew skyward. And it waxed larger as it
flew. Yet it left not my heart.

*   *   *

O my faith, my untamed knowledge, how shall I fly to your height and see with you man's larger self pencilled upon the sky?

How shall I turn this sea within me into mist and move with you in space immeasurable?

How can a prisoner within the temple behold its golden domes?

How shall the heart of a fruit be stretched to envelop the fruit also?

O my faith, I am in chains behind these bars of silver and ebony, and I cannot fly with you.

Yet out of my heart you rise skyward, and it is my heart that holds you, and I shall be content.

'Said a sheet of snow-white paper ...'

SAID A sheet of snow-white paper, 'Pure was I created, and pure will I remain for ever. I would rather be burnt and turn to white ashes than suffer darkness to touch me or the unclean to come near me'.

The ink-bottle heard what the paper was saying and it laughed in its dark heart; but it never dared to approach her. And the multicoloured pencils heard her also, and they too never came near her.

And the snow-white sheet of paper did remain pure and chaste for ever – pure and chaste – and empty.

FROM *THE PROPHET*

1923

On marriage

Then Almitra spoke again and said, and what of Marriage,
master?
And he answered saying:
You were born together, and together you shall be forever-
more.
You shall be together, when the white wings of death scatter
your days.
Ay, you shall be together even in the silent memory of God.
But let there be spaces in your togetherness,
And let the winds of the heavens dance between you.

Love one another, but make not a bond of love:
Let it rather be a moving sea between the shores of your souls.
Fill each other's cup but drink not from one cup.
Give one another of your bread but eat not from the same loaf.
Sing and dance together and be joyous, but let each one of you
be alone,
Even as the strings of a lute are alone though they quiver with
the same music.

Give your hearts, but not into each other's keeping.
For only the hand of Life can contain your hearts.

And stand together yet not too near together:
For the pillars of the temple stand apart,
And the oak tree and the cypress grow not in each other's shadow.

On children

And a woman who held a babe against her bosom said, Speak
to us of Children.
And he said:
Your children are not your children.
They are the sons and daughters of Life's longing for itself.
They come through you but not from you,
And though they are with you yet they belong not to you.

You may give them your love but not your thoughts,
For they have their own thoughts.
You may house their bodies but not their souls,
For their souls dwell in the house of tomorrow, which you
cannot visit, not even in your dreams.
You may strive to be like them, but seek not to make them like you.
For life goes not backward nor tarries with yesterday.

You are the bows from which your children as living arrows are
sent forth.
The archer sees the mark upon the path of the infinite, and
He bends you with His might that His arrows may go swift
and far.
Let your bending in the archer's hand be for gladness;
For even as He loves the arrow that flies, so He loves also the
bow that is stable.

On reason and passion

And the priestess spoke again and said: Speak to us of Reason
and Passion.
And he answered, saying:
Your soul is oftentimes a battlefield, upon which your reason
and your judgment wage war against your passion and your
appetite.

Would that I could be the peacemaker in your soul, that I might turn the discord and rivalry of your elements into oneness and melody.

But how shall I, unless you yourselves be the peacemakers, nay, the lovers of all your elements?

Your reason and your passion are the rudder and the sails of your seafaring soul.

If either your sails or your rudder be broken, you can but toss and drift, or else be held at a standstill in mid-sea.

For reason, ruling alone, is a force confining; and passion, unattended, is a flame that burns to its own destruction.

Therefore let your soul exalt your reason to the height of passion, that it may sing;

And let it direct your passion with reason, that your passion may live through its own daily resurrection, and like the phoenix rise above its own ashes.

I would have you consider your judgment and your appetite even as you would two loved guests in your house.

Surely you would not honour one guest above the other; for he who is more mindful of one loses the love and the faith of both.

Among the hills, when you sit in the cool shade of the white poplars, sharing the peace and serenity of distant fields and meadows – then let your heart say in silence, 'God rests in reason.'

And when the storm comes and the mighty wind shakes the forest and thunder and lightning proclaim the majesty of the sky, – then let your heart say in awe, 'God moves in passion.'

And since you are a breath in God's sphere and a leaf in God's forest, you too should rest in reason and move in passion.

FROM *SAND AND FOAM*

1926

I am for ever walking upon these shores,
Betwixt the sand and the foam.
The high tide will erase my foot-prints,
And the wind will blow away the foam.
But the sea and the shore will remain
For ever.

*

It was but yesterday I thought myself a fragment quivering
without rhythm in the sphere of life.
Now I know that I am the sphere, and all life in rhythmic frag-
ments moves within me.

*

They say to me in their awakening, 'You and the world you
live in are but a grain of sand upon the infinite shore of an
infinite sea.'
And in my dream I say to them, 'I am the infinite sea, and all
worlds are but grains of sand upon my shore.'

*

Only once have I been made mute. It was when a man asked
me, 'Who are you?'

*

Once I saw the face of a woman and I beheld all her children
not yet born.

And a woman looked upon my face and she knew all my
forefathers, dead before she was born.

*

A pearl is a temple built by pain around a grain of sand.

*

Remembrance is a form of meeting.

*

Forgetfulness is a form of freedom.

*

Make me, O God, the prey of the lion, ere You make the
rabbit my prey.

*

One may not reach the dawn save by the path of the night.

*

You are blind and I am deaf and dumb, so let us touch hands
and understand.

*

The significance of man is not in what he attains, but rather in
what he longs to attain.

*

Some of us are like ink and some like paper.

And if it were not for the blackness of some of us, some of us
would be dumb.

And if it were not for the whiteness of some of us, some of us
would be blind.

*

The reality of the other person is not in what he reveals to you,
but in what he cannot reveal to you.

*

The real in us is silent; the acquired is talkative.

*

Frogs may bellow louder than bulls, but they cannot drag the plough in the field nor turn the wheel of the winepress and of their skins you cannot make shoes.

*

Many a doctrine is like a window pane. We see truth through it, but it divides us from truth.

*

How noble is the sad heart who would sing a joyous song with joyous hearts.

*

Every man loves two women; the one is the creation of his imagination, and the other is not yet born.

*

Men who do not forgive women their little faults will never enjoy their great virtues.

*

Love that does not renew itself every day becomes a habit and in turn a slavery.

*

Love is a word of light, written by a hand of light, upon a page of light.

*

How shall my heart be unsealed unless it be broken?

*

Generosity is not in giving me that which I need more than you do, but it is in giving me that which you need more than I do.

*

You are indeed charitable when you give, and while giving turn your face away so that you may not see the shyness of the receiver.

FROM *JESUS,*
THE SON OF MAN
1928

Mary Magdalen

I T WAS in the month of June when I saw Him for the first time. He was walking in the wheat-field when I passed by with my handmaidens and He was alone.

The rhythm of His step was different from other men's and the movement of His body was like naught I had seen before.

Men do not pace the earth in that manner. And even now I do not know whether He walked fast or slow.

My handmaidens pointed their fingers at Him and spoke in shy whispers to one another. And I stayed my steps for a moment and raised my hand to hail Him. But He did not turn His face and He did not look at me. And I hated Him. I was swept back into myself and I was as cold as if I had been in a snow-drift. And I shivered.

That night I beheld Him in my dreaming; and they told me afterward that I screamed in my sleep and was restless upon my bed.

It was in the month of August that I saw Him again, through my window. He was sitting in the shadow of the cypress tree across my garden, and He was as still as if He had been carved out of stone, like the statues in Antioch and other cities of the North Country.

And my slave, the Egyptian, came to me said: 'That man is here again. He is sitting there across your garden.'

And I gazed at Him, and my soul quivered within me, for He was beautiful.

His body was single and each part seemed to love every other part.

Then I clothed myself with the raiment of Damascus, and I left my house and walked towards Him.

Was it my aloneness, or was it His fragrance, that drew me to Him? Was it a hunger in my eyes that desired comeliness, or was it His beauty that sought the light of my eyes?

Even now I do not know.

I walked to Him with my scented garments and my golden sandals, the sandals the Roman captain had given me, even these sandals. When I reached Him, I said: 'Good morrow to you'.

And He said: 'Good morrow to you, Miriam'.

And He looked at me, and His night-eyes saw me as no man had seen me. And suddenly I was as if naked, and I was shy.

Yet He had only said: 'Good morrow to you'.

And then I said to Him: 'Will you not come to my house?'

And He said: 'Am I not already in your house?'

I did not know what He meant then, but I know now.

And I said: 'Will you not have wine and bread with me?'

And He said: 'Yes, Miriam, but not now'.

Not now, not now, He said. And the voice of the sea was in those two words, and the voice of the wind and the trees. And when He said them unto me, life spoke to death.

For mind you, my friend, I was dead. I was a woman who had divorced her soul. I was living apart from this self which you now see. I belonged to all men, and to none. They called me harlot, and a woman possessed of seven devils. I was cursed, and I was envied.

But when His dawn-eyes looked into my eyes all the stars of my night faded away, and I became Miriam, only Miriam, a woman lost to the earth she had known, and finding herself in new places.

And now again I said to Him: 'Come into my house and share bread and wine with me'.

And He said: 'Why do you bid me to be your guest?'

And I said: 'I beg you to come into my house'. And it was all that was sod in me and all that was sky in me calling unto Him.

Then He looked at me, and the noontide of His eyes was upon me and He said: 'You have many lovers and yet I alone love you. Other men love themselves in your nearness. I love you in your self. Other men see a beauty in you that shall fade away sooner than their own years. But I see in you a beauty that shall not fade away and in the autumn of your days that beauty shall not be afraid to gaze at itself in the mirror, and it shall not be offended.

'I alone love the unseen in you'.

Then He said in a low voice: 'Go away now. If this cypress tree is yours and you would not have me sit in its shadow, I will walk my way'.

And I cried to Him and I said: 'Master, come to my house. I have incense to burn for you, and a silver basin for your feet. You are a stranger and yet not a stranger. I entreat you, come to my house'.

Then He stood up and looked at me even as the seasons might look down upon the fields, and He smiled. And He said again: 'All men love you for themselves. I love you for yourself'.

And then He walked away.

But no other man ever walked the way He walked. Was it a breath born in my garden that moved to the east? Or was it a storm that would shake all things to their foundations?

I knew not, but on that day the sunset of His eyes slew the dragon in me and I became a woman, I became Miriam, Miriam of Mijdel.

Rumanous, a Greek poet

H E WAS a poet. He saw for our eyes and heard for our ears and our silent words were upon His lips; and His fingers touched what we could not feel.

Out of His heart there flew countless singing birds to the north and to the south and the little flowers on the hillsides stayed His steps towards the heavens.

Oftentimes I have seen Him bending down to touch the blades of grass. And in my heart I have heard Him say: 'Little green things, you shall be with me in my kingdom, even as the oaks of Besan, and the cedars of Lebanon'.

He loved all things of loveliness, the shy faces of children, and the myrrh and frankincense from the south.

He loved a pomegranate or a cup of wine given Him in kindness; it mattered not whether it was offered by a stranger in the inn or by a rich host.

And He loved the almond blossoms. I have seen Him gathering them into His hands and covering His face with the petals, as though He would embrace with His love all the trees in the world.

He knew the sea and the heavens; and He spoke of pearls which have light that is not of this light, and of stars that are beyond our night.

He knew the mountains as eagles know them, and the valleys as they are known by the brooks and the streams. And there was a desert in His silence and a garden in His speech.

Aye, He was a poet whose heart dwelt in a bower beyond the heights, and His songs though sung for our ears, were sung for other ears also, and to men in another land where life is for ever young and time is always dawn.

Once I too deemed myself a poet, but when I stood before Him in Bethany, I knew what it is to hold an instrument with but a single string before one who commands all instruments. For in His voice there was the laughter of thunder and the tears of rain, and the joyous dancing of trees in the wind.

And since I have known that my lyre has but one string, and that my voice weaves neither the memories of yesterday nor the hopes of tomorrow, I have put aside my lyre and I shall keep silence. But always at twilight I shall hearken, and I shall listen to the Poet who is the sovereign of all poets.

FROM *THE EARTH GODS*

1931

[*I could not but choose the hardest way*]

Second God

I would not be so vain as to be no more.
I could not but choose the hardest way; [...]
To raise man from secret darkness,
Yet keep his roots clinging to the earth;
To give him thirst for life, and make death his cup-bearer;
To endow him with love that waxeth with pain,
And exalts with desire, and increases with longing,
And fadeth away with the first embrace;
To girdle his nights with dreams of higher days,
And infuse his days with visions of blissful nights,
And yet to confine his days and his nights
To their immutable resemblance;
To make his fancy like the eagle of the mountain,
And his thought as the tempest of the seas,
And yet to give him hands slow in decision,
And feet heavy with deliberation;
To give him gladness that he may sing before us,
And sorrow that he may call unto us,
And then to lay him low,

When the earth in her hunger cries for food;
To raise his soul high above the firmament
That he may foretaste our tomorrow,
And to keep his body grovelling in the mire
That he may not forget his yesterday.

Thus shall we rule man unto the end of time,
Governing the breath that began with his mother's crying,
And ends with the lamentation of his children.

[*Let love, human and frail, command the coming day*]

First God

Let the singer cry, and the dancer whirl her feet
And let me be content awhile.
Let my soul be serene this night.
Perchance I may drowse, and drowsing
Behold a brighter world
And creatures more starry supple to my mind.

Third God

Now I will rise and strip me of time and space,
And I will dance in that field untrodden,
And the dancer's feet will move with my feet;
And I will sing in that higher air,
And a human voice will throb within my voice.

We shall pass into the twilight;
Perchance to wake to the dawn of another world.
But love shall stay,
And his finger-marks shall not be erased.

The blessed forge burns,
The sparks rise, and each spark is a sun.
Better it is for us, and wiser,
To seek a shadowed nook and sleep in our earth divinity,
And let love, human and frail, command the coming day.

FROM *THE WANDERER*

1932

The wanderer

I MET HIM at the crossroads, a man with but a cloak and a staff and a veil of pain upon his face. And we greeted one another and I said to him, 'Come to my house and be my guest'.

And he came.

My wife and my children met us at the threshold and he smiled at them, and they loved his coming.

Then we all sat together at the board and we were happy with the man for there was a silence and a mystery in him.

And after supper we gathered to the fire and I asked him about his wanderings.

He told us many a tale that night and also the next day, but what I now record was born out of the bitterness of his days though he himself was kindly and these tales are of the dust and patience of his road.

And when he left us after three days we did not feel that a guest had departed but rather that one of us was still out in the garden and had not yet come in.

Peace and war

THREE DOGS were basking in the sun and conversing. The first dog said dreamily, 'It is indeed wondrous to be living in this day of dogdom. Consider the ease with which we travel under the sea, upon the earth and even in the sky. And meditate for a moment upon the inventions brought forth for the comfort of dogs, even for our eyes and ears and noses'.

And the second dog spoke and he said, 'We are more heedful of the arts. We bark at the moon more rhythmically than did our forefathers. And when we gaze at ourselves in the water we see that our features are clearer than the features of yesterday'.

Then the third dog spoke and said, 'But what interests me most and beguiles my mind is the tranquil understanding existing between dogdoms'.

At that very moment they looked, and lo, the dog-catcher was approaching.

The three dogs sprang up and scampered down the street; and as they ran the third dog said, 'For God's sake, run for your lives. Civilization is after us'.

The quest

A THOUSAND YEARS ago two philosophers met on a slope of Lebanon and one said to the other, 'Where goest thou?'.

And the other answered, 'I am seeking after the fountain of youth which I know wells out among these hills. I have found writings which tell of that fountain flowering toward the sun. And you, what are you seeking?'.

The first man answered, 'I am seeking after the mystery of death'.

Then each of the two philosophers conceived that the other was lacking in his great science, and they began to wrangle, and to accuse each other of spiritual blindness.

Now while the two philosophers were loud upon the wind, a stranger, a man who was deemed a simpleton in his own village, passed by and when he heard the two in hot dispute, he stood awhile and listened to their argument.

Then he came near to them and said, 'My good men, it seems that you both really belong to the same school of philosophy and that you are speaking of the same thing, only you speak in different words. One of you seeks the fountain of youth, and the other seeks the mystery of death. Yet indeed they are but one and as one they dwell in you both'.

Then the stranger turned away saying, 'Farewell, sages'. And as he departed he laughed a patient laughter.

The two philosophers looked at each other in silence for a moment, and then they laughed also. And one of them said, 'Well now, shall we not walk and seek together'?

The river

IN THE valley of Kadisha where the mighty river flows, two little streams met and spoke to one another.

One stream said, 'How came you, my friend and how was your path?'.

And the other answered, 'My path was most encumbered. The wheel of the mill was broken, and the master farmer who used to conduct me from my channel to his plants, is dead. I struggled down oozing with the filth of those who do naught but sit and bake their laziness in the sun. But how was your path, my brother'?

And the other stream answered and said, 'Mine was a different path. I came down the hills among fragrant flowers and shy willows; men and women drank of me with silvery cups and little children paddled their rosy feet at my edges and there was laughter all about me and there were sweet songs. What a pity that your path was not so happy'.

At that moment the river spoke with a loud voice and said, 'Come in, come in, we are going to the sea. Come in, come in, speak no more. Be with me now. We are going to the sea. Come in, come in, for in me you shall forget your wanderings, sad or gay. Come in, come in. And you and I will forget all our ways when we reach the heart of our mother the sea'.

FROM *THE GARDEN OF THE PROPHET*

1933

[*Pity the nation ...*]

... And on a morning his disciples sat around him and there were distances and remembrances in his eyes. And that disciple who was called Hafiz said unto him: 'Master, tell us of the city of Orphalese and of that land wherein you tarried those twelve years'.

And Almustafa was silent and he looked away toward the hills and toward the vast ether and there was a battle in his silence.

Then he said: 'My friends and my road-fellows, pity that nation that is full of beliefs and empty of religion.

'Pity the nation that wears a cloth it does not weave, eats a bread it does not harvest, and drinks a wine that flows not from its own wine-press.

'Pity the nation that acclaims the bully as hero and that deems the glittering conqueror bountiful.

'Pity the nation that despises a passion in its dream, yet submits in its awakening.

'Pity the nation that raises not its voice save when it walks in a funeral, boasts not except among its ruins and will rebel not save when its neck is laid between the sword and the block.

'Pity the nation whose statesman is a fox, whose philosopher is a juggler, and whose art is the art of patching and mimicking.

'Pity the nation that welcomes its new ruler with trumpetings, and farewells him with hootings, only to welcome another with trumpetings again.

'Pity the nation whose sages are dumb with years and whose strong men are yet in the cradle.

'Pity the nation divided into fragments, each fragment deeming itself a nation'.

[*O mist, my wingèd sister*]

And now it was eventide.

And he had reached the hills. His steps had led him to the mist, and he stood among the rocks and the white cypress-trees hidden from all things and he spoke and said:

'O Mist, my sister, white breath not yet held in a mould,
I return to you, a breath white and voiceless,
A word not yet uttered.

'O Mist, my wingèd sister Mist, we are together now,
And together we shall be till life's second day,
Whose dawn shall lay you, dewdrops in a garden,
And me a babe upon the breast of a woman,
And we shall remember.

'O Mist, my sister, I come back, a heart listening in its depths,
Even as your heart,
A desire throbbing and aimless even as your desire,
A thought not yet gathered, even as your thought.

'O Mist, my sister, first-born of my mother,
My hands still hold the green seeds you bade me scatter,
And my lips are sealed upon the song you bade me sing;
And I bring you no fruit and I bring you no echoes,
For my hands were blind and my lips unyielding.

'O Mist, my sister, much did I love the world and the world
   loved me, for all my smiles were upon her lips and all her
   tears were in my eyes.
Yet there was between us a gulf of silence which she would not
   abridge
And I could not overstep.

'O Mist, my sister, my deathless sister Mist,
I sang the ancient songs unto my little children,
And they listened and there was wondering upon their
   face;
But tomorrow perchance they will forget the song,
And I know not to whom the wind will carry the song,
And though it was not mine own, yet it came to my heart
And dwelt for a moment upon my lips.

'O Mist, my sister, though all this came to pass,
I am at peace.
It was enough to sing to those already born.
And though the singing is indeed not mine,
Yet it is of my heart's deepest desire.

'O Mist, my sister, my sister Mist,
I am one with you now.
No longer am I a self.
The walls have fallen,
And the chains have broken;
I rise to you, a mist,
And together we shall float upon the sea until life's second
   day,
When dawn shall lay you, dewdrops in a garden,
And me a babe upon the breast of a woman'.

THREE LEBANESE
FOLK POEMS
TRANSLATED
FROM THE ARABIC
BY GIBRAN

O mother mine (Moulaya)

O mother mine, spread me the silken sheet,
And let me lie down and cover me with rose leaves.
For love-sick am I and flames of love consume me.
And if I die tomorrow, Mother, I beseech you
Call round me my comrades, the daughters of love,
And over my bier let them sing me my dirge.

O mother mine, yesterday our secret was our own;
Today who does not know it?
My love has gone afar,
And now I would write to him.
If you deny me paper, I'll write on wings of birds;
And if ink you deny me, I'll write with my heart's blood!

O you, who are climbing the mountain,
A drink will you not give me from the hollow of your hand?
In truth, I am not thirsty,
But I would have a word with you;
And it may be the wind will lift your scarf
And let me look full at your face!

I wandered among the mountains

I wandered among the mountains searching for my lark,
And I found him, but alas! In another maiden's cage.
With the tinkling of gold I sought to lure him into my cage;
But she sang and said, 'Go your way. Your day is forever by'.

They said to me, 'Your love is ill and wasted, and tomorrow he
    will die'.
Then to a carpenter I went and ordered a coffin
Whose lock is of gold and whose key of a ruby carved;
And tomorrow, how astonished the kingdom will be
When they behold two youths in but a single coffin!

My love now wears a black shirt woven of hair.
Like thorns it wounds his skin
Luckless may the weaver be;
And restless, the dyer!
Some day I shall seek the head of the monastery
And plead for my love;
Then I shall tell him that one glimpse of love
Is holier than all monasteries.

Who among you has not loved?
In what heart does God not walk?
See how close are the pomegranate seeds;
And behold the stars how near and loving!
Be quiet, my heart and weep no more.
He has forgotten you;
Forget him, too. But should you forget him,
Then will I tear you out of my bosom!

O dark one, how often have I been blamed for your sake;
And each time I am blamed, my love grows stronger.
You are the rose and I, the dew that refreshes you;
You are the silken garments and I, the wind that moves you;
You are the Pleiades and I Orion, following you;
You are the moon and I, the stars that watch over you.

Three maiden lovers

Three maiden lovers stood by the wine-press.
One longed silently for her lover, who was distant

The second one said, 'All will be well'.
'Ah, well', said the third, 'but is not love God?'.

Yester-eve she was reaping with me in the corn,
And in her hair the wind played gaily.

O ye poor, pitiful mate-less things!
Your bread is but thistles and sour grapes, your wine!

My love took her basket to gather the herbs,
And all through the village she sought her mate for a
   companion;

And finding him not, she threw down her basket and said,
'Burn thou up and let they flames rise, a sacrifice to God!'.

SELECTIONS FROM
THE LETTERS

MISCELLANEOUS LETTERS

Translated by A R Ferris

To Ameen Guraieb
Boston, 12th February 1908

Only my sister Miriana knows something about this bit of news which I am going to tell you and which will make you and your neighbours rather happy: I am going to Paris, the capital of fine arts, in the late part of the coming spring, and I shall remain there one whole year. The twelve months which I am going to spend in Paris will play an important part in my everyday life, for the time which I will spend in the City of Light will be, with the help of God, the beginning of a new chapter in the story of my life. I shall join a group of great artists in that great city and work under their supervision and gain a lot from their observation and benefit myself from their constructive criticism in the field of fine arts. It matters not whether they benefit me or not, because after my return from Paris to the United States, my drawings will gain more prestige, which makes the blind-rich buy more of them, not because of their artistic beauty, but because of their being painted by an artist who has spent a full year in Paris among the great European painters.

I never dreamed of this voyage before, and the thought of it never did enter into my mind, for the expense of the trip would make it impossible for a man like me to undertake such a venture. But heaven, my dear Ameen, has arranged for this trip, without my being aware of it and opened before me the way to Paris. I shall spend one whole cycle of my life there at the expense of heaven, the source of plenty.

And now, since you have heard my story you will know that my stay in Boston is neither due to my love for this city, nor to my dislike for New York. My being here is due to the presence of a she-angel who is ushering me towards a splendid future and paving for me the path to intellectual and financial success ....

To Nakhli Gibran
Boston, 15ᵗʰ March 1908

... You know that Gibran, who spends most of his life writing, finds enchanting pleasure in corresponding with the people he loves most. You also know that Gibran, who was very fond of Nakhli when he was a child, will never forget the man that Nakhli has become. The things which the child loves remain in the domain of the heart until old age. The most beautiful thing in life is that our souls remain hovering over the places where we once enjoyed ourselves. I am one of those who remembers such places regardless of distance or time. I do not let one single phantom disappear with the cloud and it is my everlasting remembrance of the past that causes my sorrow sometimes. But if I had to choose between joy and sorrow, I would not exchange the sorrows of my heart for the joys of the whole world.

And now let me drop the curtain upon the past and tell you something about my present and my future, for I know that you would like to hear something about the boy you have always loved. Listen to me and I will read to you the first chapter of Gibran's story: I am a man of weak constitution, but my health is good because I neither think about it nor have time to worry about it. I love to smoke and drink coffee. If you were to come to see me now and enter my room, you would find me behind a screen of thick smoke mingled with the aromatic scent of Yamanite coffee.

I love to work and I do not let one moment pass without working. But the days in which I find myself dormant and my thoughtful sloth are more bitter than quinine and more severe than the teeth of the wolf. I spend my life writing and painting and my enjoyment in these two arts is above all other enjoyments. I feel that the fires that feed the affection within me would like to dress themselves with ink and paper but I am not sure whether the Arabic-speaking world would remain as friendly to me as it has been in the past three years. I say this because the apparition of enmity has already appeared. The people in Syria are calling me heretic and the intelligentsia in Egypt vilifies me, saying, 'He is the enemy of just laws, of family ties, and of old traditions'. Those writers are telling the truth, because I do not love man-made laws and I abhor the traditions that our ancestors left us. This hatred is the fruit of my love for the sacred and spiritual kindness which should be the source of every law upon the earth, for kindness is the shadow of God in man. I know that the principles upon which I base my writings are echoes of the spirit of the great majority of the people of the world, because the tendency toward a spiritual independence is to our life as the heart is to the body ... Will my teaching ever be received by the Arab world or will it die away and disappear like a shadow? ...

To Ameen Guraieb
Boston, 28th March 1908

... You are now in the other part of the great but small, globe, while I am still here. You are now in beautiful and peaceful Lebanon and I am in clamorous and noisy Boston. You are in the East and I am in the West but no matter how far away you are from me, I feel that you are closer to me than ever. Man finds the expatriation of his beloved friends difficult to bear because his pleasure comes through the five senses. But Gibran's soul has already grown beyond that to a plane of higher enjoyment which does not require the mediation of the five senses. His soul sees, hears and feels but not through the medium of eyes, ears and fingers. His soul roams the whole world and returns without the use of feet, cars and ships. I see Ameen far and near and I perceive everything around him as the soul regards many other invisible and voiceless objects. The subtlest beauties in our life are unseen and unheard.

How did you find Lebanon? Is it as beautiful as your yearnings promised? Or is it an arid spot where slothfulness dwells? Is Lebanon the same glorious Mountain whose beauty was sung and praised by poets like David, Isaiah, Farhat, Lamartine, and Haddad? Or is it a chain of mountains and valleys empty of geniality, aloof from beauty and surrounded by loneliness? ...

I used to look upon life through tears and laughter but today I see life through golden and enchanting rays of light that impart strength to the soul and courage to the heart and motion to the body. I used to be like a bird imprisoned in a cage, contenting myself with seeds dropped down to me by the hands of Destiny. But today I feel like a free bird, who sees the beauty of the fields and prairies and wishes to fly in the spacious sky, mingling its affections, its fancy and its hopes with the ether ...

When you are in a beautiful spot or among learned people or by the side of old ruins or on top of a high mountain, whisper my name so that my soul will go to Lebanon and hover around you and share with you the pleasure of life and all life's meanings and secrets. Remember me when you see the sun rising from behind Mount Sunnin or Fam El Mizab. Think of me when you see the sun coming down toward its setting, spreading its red garment upon the mountains and the valleys as if shedding blood instead of tears as it bids Lebanon farewell. Recall my name when you see the shepherds sitting in the shadow of the trees and blowing their reeds and filling the silent field with soothing music as did Apollo when he was exiled to this world. Think of me when you see the damsels carrying their earthenware jars filled with water upon their shoulders. Remember me when you see the Lebanese villager ploughing the earth before the face of the sun, with beads of sweat adorning his forehead while his back is bent under the heavy duty of labour. Remember me when you hear the songs and hymns that Nature has woven from the sinews of moonlight, mingled with the aromatic scent of the valleys, mixed with the frolicsome breeze of the Holy Cedars and poured into the hearts of the Lebanese. Remember me when the people invite you to their festivities, for your remembrance of me will bring to you pictures of my love and longing for your person and will add spiritual overtones and deeper meaning to your words and your speeches. Love and longing, my dear Ameen, are the beginning and the end of our deeds ....

To Nakhli Gibran
Paris, 27th September 1910

... On the fourteenth day of the coming month I shall leave Paris, but now I am busy arranging my work and planning for the future. I am like a spinning wheel turning day and night. God only knows how busy I am. Thus heaven directs my life and thus destiny rotates me around a certain point from which I cannot get away ....

Just think, my dear Nakhli and ponder upon Gibran's life, for it reveals to you a sort of struggle and strife. It is a chain of connected links of misery and distress. I can say these things to you because I am very patient and glad of the existence of hardships in my life, for I hope to overcome all these difficulties. Had it not been for the presence of calamities, work and struggle would not have existed and life would have been cold, barren and boresome.

To May Ziadah
1928

I am indebted for all that I call 'I' to women, ever since I was an infant. Women opened the windows of my eyes and the doors of my spirit. Had it not been for the woman-mother, the woman-sister and the woman-friend, I would have been sleeping among those who seek the tranquility of the world with their snoring.

... I have found pleasure in being ill. This pleasure differs with its effect from any other pleasure. I have found a sort of tranquility, that makes me love illness. The sick man is safe from people's strife, demands, dates and appointments, excess of talking and ringing of telephones ... I have found another kind of enjoyment through illness which is more important and unmeasurable. I have found that I am closer to abstract things in my sickness than in health. When I lay my head upon the pillow and close my eyes and lose myself to the world, I find myself flying like a bird over serene valleys and forests, wrapped in a gentle veil. I see myself close to those whom my heart has loved, calling and talking to them but without anger and with the same feelings they feel and the same thoughts they think. They lay their hands now and then upon my forehead to bless me.

... I wish I were sick in Egypt or in my country so I might be close to the ones I love*. Do you know, May, that every morning and every evening I find myself in a home in Cairo with you sitting before me reading the last article I wrote or the one you wrote which has not yet been published.

* At the writing of this letter May was living in Cairo, Egypt.

... Do you realise, May, that whenever I think of the Departure which the people call Death, I find pleasure in such thinking and great longing for such departure. But then I return to myself and remember that there is one word I must say before I depart. I become perplexed between my disability and my obligation and I give up hope. No, I have not said my word yet, and nothing but smoke has come out from this light. This is what makes me feel that cessation of work is more bitter than gall. I say this to you, May and I don't say it to anyone else: If I don't depart before I spell and pronounce my word, I will return to say the word which is now hanging like a cloud in the sky of my heart.

... Does this sound strange to you? The strangest things are the closest to the real truth. In the will of man there is a power of longing which turns the mist in ourselves into sun.

From a letter to Felix Farris
1930

... It is not strange that we are both struck by the same arrow at the same time. Pain, my brother, is an unseen and powerful hand that breaks the skin of the stone in order to extract the pulp. I am still at the mercy of the doctors and I shall remain subject to their weights and measures until my body rebels against them or my soul revolts against my body. Mutiny shall come in the form of surrender and surrender in the form of mutiny; but whether I rebel or not, I must go back to Lebanon, and I must withdraw myself from this civilisation that runs on wheels. However, I deem it wise not to leave this country before I break the strings and chains that tie me down; and numerous are those strings and those chains! I wish to go back to Lebanon and remain there forever.

FROM LETTERS TO
AMEEN RIHANI

Translated by Suheil Bushrui

Paris, 23rd August 1910

My dear Ameen,

... Since my return from London I have been entangled between lines and colours as a bird that has broken free from its cage and flown through fields and valleys. The exercises that I have done are better than anything I have done in Paris. I feel now that an invisible hand is polishing off the dust from the mirror of my soul and is tearing the veil asunder from my eyes and showing me pictures and images more clearly, nay more beautifully and gloriously. Art, Ameen, is a great god. We cannot touch the hems of his robes save with fingers purified by fire and cannot look upon his face save from behind eyelids bathed in tears.

I shall leave Paris in a few weeks and my joy will be great to find you recovered, strong as the sacred tree that grows before Astarte's temple and joyful as the whispering pond in Qadisha Valley. Until we meet, beloved friend, until we meet and may God keep you for your brother,

[Kahlil Gibran]

* * *

Boston, December 1911

My brother and co-worker Ameen,

My brother in art and my co-worker in the realm of God's Law,

Since my arrival in this city I have been among friends and acquaintances like a human being in the magical caves of the djinn where ghosts and spirits hide with the swiftness of thought. I link the end of the night with the break of day – it is a life I do not like to have too much of although it has a certain aesthetic beauty ....

I will not bid you a happy new year but will bid the new year happiness in having you and I will not wish you what people wish each other, but I will wish for people some of what you possess – for you are rich in yourself and I am rich in you. May God keep you for your brother,

[Kahlil Gibran]

* * *

12th June 1912

My brother Ameen,

... farewell before your ship takes you towards that place where the sun rises. I would have wished to accompany you to that land, the rocks and valleys of which I love and the priests and rulers of which I hate. But what dreams portray, wakefulness erases; and what hope clarifies, powerlessness hides.

On the morrow you are travelling to the most beautiful and the most sacred country in this world and I shall remain in this distant exile. How fortunate you are and how unlucky I am. If you were but to think of me on Sannin or near Byblos or in the valley of al-Fouraika, you will minimize the torment of exile and reduce the pain of separation.

There may be no one in Syria who is interested in me but there are a few individuals in whom I am interested. These are those who think a lot, speak little and feel always. To all those I send my greetings and salutations. But to those who swell like drums and croak like frogs I send nothing – not even an iota of my contempt.

And forget not, my brother the white 'abaye [Arab cloak] embroidered with gold and stop at no price but produce the best, the most beautiful, the most glorious, the most brilliant, the most splendid in Syria.

But above all recuperate and if you can, come back with another *Khalid* and remember that I shall be in New York next winter. May God protect you and keep you for your brother ...

[Kahlil Gibran]

*　*　*

Probably 1917

My brother Ameen,

God's peace be upon you. The situation here increases in confusion daily and my patience has reached its limit, for I am among a people whose language I do not understand and who do not understand mine.

Ameen Saliba has tried to annex the Philadelphia Committee to his own and he might succeed. Ni'mah Tadros never comes to this office and does not sign the receipts! Najib Shacrein has formally resigned and I am trying to placate him with all the proofs I have at hand.

Najib al-Kisbani is overwhelmed and doesn't know what he's doing.

Mr. Dodge informed us that he's going to the country and asked us to meet with Mr. Scott.

The city Mayor cannot give us permission for a tag day.

All the Syrians are much more interested today than they have been in the past – the leaders grow in their leadership while the gossip-mongers intensify their gossip-mongering.

All these matters, Ameen, have led me to hate life and had it not been for the cries of the hungry that filled my heart I would never have spent a minute longer in this office or an hour longer than I should have in this city.

Tomorrow evening we shall meet and present to the Committee the matter of contributions to the American Committee. I swear by God, Ameen, that it would be better sharing the deprivation of the hungry and the suffering of the afflicted and if I were to choose between death in Lebanon or life among these creatures I would choose death.

Enjoy the greenness of the valley, Ameen and come back to us happy and rested and may God keep you for your brother,

[Kahlil Gibran]

FROM LETTERS TO
MAY ZIADAH

Translated by Suheil Bushrui and Salma Haffar al-Kuzbari

New York, 7th February 1919

My dear Miss May,*

Your letter brought back to me 'the memory of a thousand springs and a thousand autumns', and I found myself standing once more before those ghosts which disappeared and hid in silence as soon as the volcano erupted in Europe† – what a long and profound silence it has been!

Do you know, my friend, that I used to find solace, companionship and comfort in our much interrupted dialogue? And do you know that I used to tell myself: 'There is, in the distant East, a maiden who is not like other maidens, who has entered the temple even before she was born, has stood in the Holiest of Holies and has come to know the sublime secret guarded by the "giants of the dawn". She has since adopted my country as her country and has taken my people to be her people?'. Do you know that I used to whisper this hymn in the ear of my

---

* 'Mary', was May Ziadah's original Christian name, but she chose 'May' because it was more poetic. Gibran addressed her as 'May', 'Mary', and 'Miriam' – the last being another of Gibran's adaptations of May's name.
† He is referring to the First World War.

imagination every time I received a letter from you? If you had but known, you would have never stopped writing to me – on the other hand, you may have known and that is why you stopped writing, a decision not altogether devoid of wisdom and good judgment ....

When I declare that 'Those who understand us subjugate something in us', you ask whether I would like *anyone* to understand me. No! No! I want no human being to understand me if his understanding entails my spiritual enslavement. There are many people who imagine that they understand us because they find in our 'exterior' behaviour something akin to what they have experienced but once in their lifetime. It is not enough [for them] to claim they know our secrets – the secrets which we within ourselves do not know – but they must number us and give us labels and shelve us in one of the many compartments which comprise their thoughts and ideas, just as the chemist does with his bottles of medicine and powders. The writer who claims that you imitate me in some of your writing – isn't he one of those people who claim that they understand and know our secrets? It would be impossible for you to convince him that independence is the point all souls move towards, and that the oak and the willow do not grow in each other's shade.

I have reached this point in my letter without having said one word of what I meant to say when I began. Which one of us is capable of transforming the gentle mist into statues or sculptured form? But the Lebanese maiden who hears those sounds which are beyond sound shall discern both forms and spirits in the mist.

Peace be with your beautiful soul and your great and noble heart. God protect you.

Yours sincerely,
Gibran Kahlil Gibran

* * *

New York, 25th July 1919

My dear Miss May,

You have been in my mind ever since I last wrote to you. I have spent long hours thinking of you, talking to you, endeavouring to discover your secrets, trying to unravel your mysteries. Even so, it is still surprising to me that I should have felt the presence of your ethereal [incorporeal] Self in my study, watching the moves I make, conversing and arguing with me, voicing opinions on what I do.

You will naturally be surprised to hear me talk like this; I myself find it strange that I should feel this urge and this necessity to write to you. I wish it were possible for me to comprehend the hidden secret behind this necessity, this urgent need.

You once said that 'there is always a dialectic between minds and an interplay of thoughts, [both of] which lie beyond sensory awareness; and no-one can ever entirely erase that interplay and dialectic from the minds and thoughts of those who belong to the same native land'.

In this beautiful passage resides a fundamental truth, once clear to me through a kind of mental empathy, but now clear to me through personal experience. I have recently established a bond, abstract, delicate, firm, strange and unlike all other bonds in its nature and characteristics, a bond which cannot be compared to the natural familial bonds, a bond which, indeed, is far more steadfast, firm and permanent even than moral bonds.

Not a single one of the threads which form this bond was woven by the days and nights which measure time and intersperse the distance that separates the cradle from the grave. Not a single one of those threads was woven by past interests or future aspirations – for this bond has existed between two people who were brought together by neither the past nor the present, and who may not be united by the future, either.

In such a bond, May, in such a private emotion, in such a secret understanding, there exist dreams more exotic and more unfathomable than anything that surges in the human breast; dreams within dreams within dreams.

Such an understanding, May, is a deep and silent song which is heard in the stillness of the night; it transports us beyond the realms of day, beyond the realms of night, beyond time, beyond eternity.

Such an emotion, May, involves sharp pangs that will never disappear but which are dear to us, and which we would not exchange, even if we had the chance, for any amount of glory or pleasure, known or imagined.

The above is an attempt to communicate to you that which cannot be communicated to you by anyone other than him who shares in all that is within you. If, therefore, I have fathomed a secret with which you yourself are not unacquainted, then I am one of those to whom Life has granted her gifts and permitted to stand before the White Throne but if I have fathomed that which is peculiar to me and in myself alone, then let the fire consume this letter.

I implore you, my friend, to write to me; and I implore you to write in that free, detached, winged spirit that soars far above the ways of mankind. You and I know a great deal about mankind, about the interests that bring people together and about the facts that drive them apart.

May we not withdraw a while from those well-worn paths and may we not pause for a time to gaze into the realms which lie beyond night, beyond day, beyond time, beyond eternity?

May God keep you, May and may he protect you always.

Your true friend,
Gibran Kahlil Gibran

* * *

Boston, 11ᵗʰ January 1921

May,

We have reached a mountain-top and below us are spread plains, forests and valleys, so let us sit awhile and talk a little. We cannot stay here very long because in the distance I see a higher peak, which we must reach before sunset, but we shall not leave this place until you are happy, nor take a single step forward until you have peace of mind.

We have surmounted a formidable obstacle, not without a certain amount of confusion and I confess that I have been persistent and over-pressing, but my persistence was the foreseeable result of something stronger than so-called will. I also confess that I have acted without wisdom in certain matters – are there not spheres of life which are beyond the reach of wisdom? Do we not have in us something before which wisdom turns to stone? Were my present experiences in any way like those of the past I would not have described them – but they are all strange and new and have come all of a sudden.

And had I been in Cairo and said this to you simply by word of mouth, in that detached manner without a trace of selfish ends, no misunderstanding would have arisen between us. But I was not in Cairo at that time and there was no means of communication with you other than by letter – and writing letters on subjects such as these tends to complicate the simplest of issues and throw a heavy veil of formality over the most elemental of matters. For how often, when we want to express a simple thought, do we put it in whatever words come to us, words such as our pens are accustomed to pouring out on paper and the result is usually a 'prose poem' or a 'reflective essay'. The reason for this is that we feel and think in a language that is more honest and more sincere than the language in which we write. Of course we like poems, be they in prose or in verse and we like essays both reflective and non-reflective. But free, undying passion is one thing; letter-writing is something quite else. Ever since my schooldays I have tried as far as possible to avoid using platitudes because I felt – and still feel – that they obscure both thoughts and feelings much more than they ever express them. But it appears to me now that I have not altogether escaped the very thing I abhor – it seems to me that the year and a half which has passed finds me still where I was at the age of fifteen, proof of which lies in this misunderstanding which may have resulted from my letters.

I repeat that had I been in Cairo we should have reflected awhile upon the meaning of our personal experiences as we might upon the sea or the stars or a blossoming apple-tree. For no matter how strange and unique our experiences, they are no wise more strange and unique than the sea, the stars and the blossoming apple-tree. Strange that we should accept the miracles of the earth and of space, but at the same time tend not to believe the miracles that are wrought in our souls.

I used to think, May, indeed I still think that some of our experiences cannot occur unless two people share in them jointly and simultaneously. This mode of thinking may have been the main reason why some of my letters have induced you into thinking that 'we must stop here'. Thank God we did not 'stop there'. For life, May, does not stop in one place and the mighty procession with all its beauty cannot but march forward from one sempiternity to another. As for you and me, for us who sanctify life and tend toward what is right, blessed, sweet and noble in life with all our being, who hunger and thirst after the permanent and everlasting in life – we do not wish to say or do anything that breeds fear or 'fills the soul with thorns and bitterness'. We are neither able nor willing to touch the sides of the altar save with hands that have been purified by fire. And when we love a thing, May, we look on love as a goal in itself and not as a means to achieve some other end; and if we show reverence and submission before the sublime, it is because we regard submission as elevation and reverence as a form of recompense. If we long for something, we consider longing a gift and a bounty in itself. We also know that the remotest matters are those most befitting and most worthy of our longing and our inclinations. In truth we two – you and I – cannot stand in the light of the sun and say: 'We must spare ourselves torment we can well do without'. We cannot do without that which infuses the soul with a sacred leaven, nor can we do without the caravan which takes us to God's city; indeed we cannot do without that which brings us nearer to our Greater Selves and reveals to us the power, mystery and wonder we have within our souls. Moreover we are capable of finding intellectual happiness in the simplest manifestations of the soul; for in a simple flower we find all the glory and beauty of spring, in the eyes of the infant suckling we find all the hope and aspiration of mankind. Yet we are unwilling to use those things nearest to us as a means to reach what lies far ahead. We are neither able nor inclined to stand in front of life and state our conditions [by saying]: 'Give us what we want or give us nothing – what we want or nothing at all.' No, May, we do not do this, because we realise that what is right and blessed and permanent in life does not follow our wishes but moves *us* according to its will. What motive could we have for revealing one of the secrets of our souls across the seven thousand miles that separate us, save the joy of revealing that secret? What other motive could we have for standing before the gates of the temple, except the glory of standing there? What motive does a bird have when it bursts into song or incense when it burns? For a lonely soul may only have limited aspirations.

How sweet are your birthday wishes to me and how delicate their fragrance. But let me tell you a little story, May and you may laugh awhile at my expense. Naseeb 'Arida, wishing to collect the articles of *A Tear and a Smile* [and publish them] in one volume – this was before the war – decided to append that assortment of meagre pieces with the article 'My Birthday', to which title he would add the [appropriate] date. As I was not in New York at the time, he began searching for my date of birth – he is an indefatigable researcher – until he eventually identified that date in the distant past and translated the English '6th January' into 'Kanoon al-Awal 6th'!* In this way he reduced the span of my lifetime by [nearly] a year and delayed the real day of my birth by a month! To this day, ever since the publication of *A Tear and a Smile*, I have enjoyed two birthday celebrations each year; the first was the result of an error in translation, though what error in the ethereal world really caused it I do not know! As for the year of which I have been robbed – God knows and you know, that I paid a heavy price for it. I paid for it with the throbs of my heart, I paid for it with seventy [ton] weights of silent pain and longing for a thing unknown – so how could I allow a mere error in a book to rob me of that one year?

I am far away from the 'valley', May. I arrived in this city – Boston – ten days ago to do some painting, and had they not sent me a parcel containing mail sent to my New York address, I should have lived through ten more days without your letter. This letter has untied a thousand knots in the rope of my life, and turned the desert of 'waiting' into gardens and orchards – for 'waiting' is the indelible etchings of time, May and I am continually in a state of 'waiting'. Sometimes it seems to me that I spend my life in expectation of that which has not yet come to pass – how like the blind and disabled who were lying by the pool at Bethesda in Jerusalem: 'For an angel went down at a certain season into the pool and troubled the water: whosoever then first after the troubling of the water stepped in was made whole of whatsoever disease he had'.† However, now that my own angel has troubled the waters in the pool and I have found someone to put me into those waters, I walk in that enchanted and awe-inspiring spot, my eyes filled with light and my feet strengthened with firm resolve. I walk side by side with a shadow more beautiful and more lucid than the reality of all men. I walk [with my hand] holding a hand that is silken and yet strong, with a will of its own; a hand whose fingers are soft and yet capable of lifting weights and breaking heavy chains. And every now and then I turn my

---

* *Kanoon al-Awal* (literally 'the 1st Kanoon') is the month of December, and January is *Kanoon al-Awal* (literally, 'the 2nd Kanoon').
† The reference is to the Gospel of St. John V: 4.

head to behold a pair of glittering eyes and lips touched by a smile that wounds with its sweetness.

I once told you that my life is divided into two lives and that I spend the one in working and being with people, the other in the mist. But that was yesterday, for now my life has been unified and I work in the mist, meet people in the mist, even sleep, dream and wake up in the mist. It is indeed an ecstasy surrounded by the beating of wings, for in that state of ecstasy loneliness is *not* loneliness and the pain of longing for the unknown is more pleasant than anything I have known. It is a divine trance, May – a divine trance which brings near that which is remote, uncovers that which is hidden and illuminates all things. I realise that life without this spiritual trance is but the chaff without the wheat and I aver that all we say, do or think is worthless when compared to a single minute spent in the mist.

You want the words 'lyric poem' etched on my heart! You want to use this against me so that you may take revenge against this frail form of which I am the carrier and the carried. Let it etch and etch and etch, then and let us invoke all the lyric poems that are embedded in the ether and let us command them to spread out over this 'land' and dig canals, build roads, erect palaces, towers and temples, turn the wilderness into gardens and vineyards because a mighty people are come to inhabit it and have chosen it as their home. You, May, are a great and mighty nation of conquerors and at the same time you are a little girl of seven, laughing in the sun's rays, chasing butterflies, gathering rose-buds and leaping over streams. Nothing in life is sweeter to me than running after that sweet little girl, catching her and giving her a piggy-back home so that I can tell her tales that are strange and full of wonder – until slumber touches her eyelids and she falls asleep in quiet and heavenly fashion.

Gibran

* * *

New York, 12th January 1925

Mary,

On the sixth of this month I was thinking of you every minute and every second and I was translating all that was said to me into the language of Mary and Gibran – a language which not one of the inhabitants of this earth can understand except Mary and Gibran ... and you, of course, know that every day of the year is the birthday of each one of us.

The Americans are, of all peoples in the world, the most fond of celebrating birthdays and of sending and receiving birthday presents. And for a reason that has escaped me, the Americans shower their kindness on me on such occasions. On the sixth of this month I was embarrassed by their overwhelming kindness and filled with a deep sense of gratitude. But God knows the word I received from you was far dearer and more precious to me than anything and everything others can do for me. God knows that and your heart knows it too.

After the celebrations we sat together, you and I, apart from the others and talked at length, saying to each other what cannot be spoken except by longing and speaking what cannot be said except without hope. Then we gazed up at our distant star and were silent. After that we resumed our talk until the dawn of day and your hand was placed on my throbbing heart until the morning broke.

May God watch over you and protect you, Miriam and may He shower you with His light. May God keep you for him who loves you.

Gibran

[*At the end of this letter Gibran drew the sketch of the hand below the flame that became the symbol of his love for May.*]

FROM LETTERS TO
MARY HASKELL

Paris, 8th November 1908

When I am unhappy, dear Mary, I read your letters. When the mist overwhelms the 'I' in me, I take two or three letters out of the little box and re-read them. They remind me of my true self. They make me overlook all that is not high and beautiful in life. Each and every one of us, dear Mary, must have a resting place somewhere. The resting place of my soul is a beautiful grove where my knowledge of you lives.

And now I am wrestling with colour: the strife is terrible, one of us must triumph! I can almost hear you saying, 'And what about drawing, Kahlil?' and Kahlil, with a thirst in his voice says, 'Let me, O let me bathe my soul in colours; let me swallow the sunset and drink the rainbow'.

The professors in the academy say, 'Do not make the model more beautiful than she is' and my soul whispers, 'O if you could only paint the model as beautiful as she really is'. Now what shall I do, dear Mary? Shall I please the professors or my soul? The dear old men know a great deal but the soul is much nearer.

It is rather late and I shall go to bed now, with many thoughts in my heart. Good night, dear Mary. God bless you always.

Kahlil

* * *

New York, 31st October 1911

Mary, beloved Mary, I have been downtown, among my countrymen, all day long, working hard and thinking harder. It is rather late and I am tired but I could not go to bed without saying good night to you. You have been so near – so very near me today and yesterday. Your last letter is a flame, a winged globe, a wave from That Island of strange music.

These days, beloved Mary, are full of images and voices and shadows – there is fire in my heart – there is fire in my hands – and wherever I go I see mysterious things.

Do you not know what it is to burn and burn and to know while burning, that you are freeing yourself from everything around you? Oh, there is no greater joy than the joy of Fire!

And now let me cry out with all the voices in me that I love you.

Kahlil

* * *

New York, 10th March 1912

Mary, dearest Mary, how could you, in the name of Allah, ask me if my seeing you gives me more pain than pleasure? What is there in heaven or on earth to inspire such a thought?

What is pain and what is pleasure? (Could you separate one from the other?) The power which moves you and me is composed of both pleasure and pain and that which is really beautiful gives nothing but delicious pain or painful joy.

Mary, you give me so much of a pleasure that it is painful and you give me so much of pain too and that is why I love you.

Kahlil

* * *

New York, 8th October 1913

Beloved Mary, I have lived much during the last three weeks. I have crossed an ocean and I am now in a new land. Things seem so strangely different. I am tired of the world. Why should any lover of life put up with such a stupid, soft-headed world? Someday I'll take a paintbox and a bottle of ink and go off and be a hermit. A true hermit goes to the wilderness to find not to lose himself. One can find oneself anywhere, but in large cities one must carve a way with a sword in order to see a shadow of oneself.

Just now I can't work for more than three or four hours a day. After that I need rest and space and silence. There are times when I can't work at all. Too *busy* to work. There is a form of thinking, or rather *being*, which does not permit one to do any physical work.

A volume of my earliest prose-poems is coming out in three or four weeks. I've corrected some of the proofs this morning. I hate to correct proofs. Is there anything more wearisome than examining carefully the work of one of your dead selves? It is good to be a digger of new graves, but not an inspector of old ones!

My new book is almost ready. They tell me that it must not come out too soon after the other book.

The stove hasn't come yet and I need it badly for my models.

Now, Mary, please don't think I am slow in doing things. You see, I am alone and I can't do more than one thing at a time.

Kahlil

*   *   *

New York, 28th January 1915

Beloved Mary,

I have been asleep during the past three weeks. I have thought of a thousand things which I must do this year. I fear, Mary, that I shall never be able to realize my dreams fully. I always fall short. I always get a shadow of a shadow of the thing I want.

It used to give me pleasure to hear people praising my work – but now I am strangely saddened by praise, because praise reminds me of things not yet done – and somehow I want to be loved for what I have not done yet. I know that this sounds rather childish, but how can one help wanting what one wants? Last night I said to myself, 'The physical consciousness of a plant in midwinter is not directed towards the past summer but toward the coming spring. The physical memory of a plant is not that of days that are *no more* but of days that *will be*. If plants are certain of a coming spring, through which they will come out of themselves, why cannot I, a human plant, be certain of a spring to come, in which I will be able to fulfill myself?'.

Perhaps our spring is not in this life, Mary. This life may be nothing but a winter.

K

OTHERS ON GIBRAN
THE MAN,
THE POET AND
THE ARTIST

GIBRAN: THE MAN

Mary Haskell

314 Marlboro
Wednesday, 12th June, 1912

... He sleeps now seven or eight hours out of the twenty-four. No matter whether from 12–8; or from 4–11; just so he gets it – though doctors tell him to choose the earlier hours. He does his best work between 12 and 4 at night.

He eats *very* little. 'Work and food don't go together, I find'. An orange for breakfast – and a cup of Turkish coffee – or only the coffee. No lunch or a bit of bread and cup of coffee – or just coffee – or a piece of fruit. A dinner that would be small for anyone else. And no more. Nothing between meals – just indifferent to it. And absolutely indifferent to every virtue of service except cleanliness. It is his only stipulation. Katie's* casting of food on table suits him just as well as the service given at Miss Jean's. Actually, the less service the better. So only it be clean. You can't talk him into caring about unessentials in anything.

* * *

* Maid at 314 Marlboro Street.

314 Marlboro St.
Saturday, 15th June, 1912

We met in the library. Kahlil was waiting – always there first! – reading by the table lamp – his head the most vibrant spot in the room – dark, domed, luminous – eyebrows like black lifted wings – the full high forehead – the burning star, and night quality dominant in his quietness. Lustre. – Katie, a fine dear girl, said of him yesterday, 'His face is full of stars. There's brightness all over it. Look at him and you'd know there's not a dead spot in him. Anywhere you'd see him you'd know there was a peculiar power in him and a peculiar beauty'.

C F Bragdon

I REMEMBER VIVIDLY my first meeting with Kahlil Gibran. It occurred at one of those cultural tea parties so dear to the heart of the average American woman and so abhorrent to husbands, sons and lovers. As a result the atmosphere was pervasively, even oppressively, feminine, inducing a psychic mood analogous to the physical sensation of immersion in warm water or the feel of an old-fashioned feather bed. In the waning afternoon he and I were the only two remaining, which may be the reason why, metaphorically speaking, we so fell on one another's necks.

I do not think that at that time I had really read him, though I probably pretended that I had done so, as he possibly pretended that he had done the same by me. But this proved to be a matter of no import-ance: we came together 'like kinsmen met a-night', finding that we spoke so much the same language that there was scarcely need of speech at all.

In that first meeting I saw him as I now see him, all later encounters having only deepened and intensified the impression received then. Three words describe him: *artist*, *poet*, *prophet*, though they should only be one word but this the English language fails to furnish forth.

Juliet Thompson

I T WAS on 6th April 1943, in her studio-room, upstairs at the front of the house, that Juliet shared with me and a few other guests, these memories of Kahlil Gibran.

'He lived across the street from here', said Juliet Thompson, 'at 51 West 10th. He was neither poor nor rich – in between. Worked on an Arab newspaper; free to paint and write. His health was all right in the early years. He was terribly sad in the later years, because of cancer. He died at forty-nine. He knew his life was ending too soon.

'His drawings were more beautiful than his paintings. These were very misty, lost things – mysterious and lost. Very poetic.

'A Syrian brought him to see me – can't even remember his name. Kahlil always said I was his first friend in New York. We became very, very great friends and all of his books – *The Madman, The Forerunner, The Son of Man, The Prophet* – I heard in manuscript. He always gave me his books. I liked *The Prophet* best. I don't believe that there was any connection between 'Abdu'l-Bahá and *The Prophet*. But he told me that when he wrote *The Son of Man* he thought of 'Abdu'l-Bahá all through. He said that he was going to write another book with 'Abdu'l-Bahá as the center and all the contemporaries of 'Abdu'l-Bahá speaking. He died before he wrote it. He told me definitely that *The Son of Man* was influenced by 'Abdu'l-Bahá.

'He wrote his books in the studio across the street. Then he would call me up and say come over and hear a chapter.

'He was from an old Syrian family. His grandfather was one of the Bishops. I think he always remained a Greek Christian.

'I've seen Armenians and Syrians kiss his hand and call him Master. It was very bad for Kahlil. He had hundreds of followers. He kept that place closed to all except his intimate friends and his work.

'He was in love with a friend of mine – but he just loved me and I loved him – but it wasn't that kind of love. He just wasn't a lover. He wasn't that kind of a man.

'He had a high, delicate voice and an almost shyly modest manner, until he came out with something thundering. I don't know how to describe him except to say he was the spitting image of Charlie Chaplin. I used to tell him so. It made him frightfully mad.

'How Gibran got in touch with the Bahá'í Cause: I'll just frankly tell you the story, just as it was. I hastened to tell him: he listened. He got hold of some of the Arabic of Bahá'u'lláh. He said it was the most stupendous literature that ever was written and that he even coined words. That there was no Arabic that even touched the Arabic of Bahá'u'lláh.

'And then Kahlil, 'The Master', got a following. He told me that he belonged to the Illuminati in Persia. He would rise up and say, "What do we need a Manifestation of God for? Each one of us can come into direct contact with God. I am in direct contact with God".

'I wouldn't say anything. I'd just let him talk.

'He wore American business clothes. Had lots of black hair, wavy.

'Time passed. I told him the Master was coming. He asked me if would request the Master to sit for him. The Master gave him one hour at 6:30 one morning. He made an outstanding head. It doesn't look like the Master – very faint likeness. Great power through the shoulders. A great radiance in the face. It's not a portrait of the Master, but it's the work of a great artist. I do consider him a great artist.

'He was very modest and retiring in his personal life. He'd never met the Master before and that began his friendship. He simply adored the Master. He was with Him whenever he could be. He would come over here to this house (48 West 10th) to see the Master. In Boston, he was often with the Master. All that's sort of blurred because it's so long ago. He told me two stories that I thought priceless: One day when he was driving with the Master in Boston, 'Abdu'l-Bahá said: "Why do they build their houses with flat roofs?". Kahlil didn't answer for a moment and then the Master answered himself: "Because they are domeless". Another time he was with the Master when two women came in. They were women of fashion and they asked trifling questions. One of them wanted to know whether she was going to be married again. The Master was pacing the floor. Drawing in his breath, expelling it, His eyes turning from side to side. When they left, "Gilded dirt!" he said.

'The Master went away and Kahlil settled down into writing his books. But he often talked of him, most sympathetically and most lovingly. But the only thing was, he couldn't accept an intermediary for himself. He wanted his direct contact.

'Then one night, years afterward, the Master's motion picture was going to be shown at the Bahá'í Center ... He sat beside me in the front row and he saw the Master come to life again for him in that picture. And he began to sob. We had asked him to speak a few words that night. When the time came for him to speak, he controlled himself and jumped up on the platform and then, my dear, still weeping before us all he said: "I declare that 'Abdu'l-Bahá is the Manifestation of God for this day!". Of course he got it wrong – but ... he was weeping and he didn't say anything more. He got down and he sat beside me and he kept on sobbing and sobbing and sobbing. Seeing the picture – it brought it all back. He took my two hands and said, "You have opened for me a door tonight". Then he fled the hall.

'I never heard anything about it again. He never referred to it again.

'Poor Kahlil! The end isn't so good. I was away. When I came back he was very sick. He asked me if I wouldn't come every day to see him. He was in bed. These were his last days. "I want to give you all I can while I can." He would pour out the story of his life. So much of it has evaporated.

'He told me: "When snow begins to fall it always wakes me up. One time at three in the morning I decided I'd like to go out and walk in the snow and get my thoughts together. So I went up to Central Park. I was walking with a little notebook in my hand. I was finishing *The Earth Gods* (an early book but his last). I was writing in my notebook in the snow. A big policeman came along".

'"Whatcha doin'?"

'"Writing".

'"Writing? Are you an Englishman?"

'"No".

'"Are you a Frenchman?"

'"No".

'"What are you?"

'"A Syrian".

'"Oh. Know anything about that Syrian – think his name is Kayleel Guibran – fellow who writes books?"

'"I think so".

'"Well, since he came into the life of our home there's never been any peace in it. I used to have a good wife. Now she don't do nuthin all day long but read that Kayleel Guibran".

'Those last days he just wept and wept and wept. His head on my shoulder. He never said he was dying. He never said a word. Except that one thing: "I want to give you all I can while I can. So come every day". His followers stayed with him. He's quite a cult. Buried in Boston.

'Large, tragic brown eyes. The eye was very important in his face. His forehead was broad – very high – very broad and he had almost a shock of black hair. Short, slender, five foot two or three. Very sensitive mouth – drooped a little at the corners. Very sad man who had a reason for it. Little black moustache, like Charlie Chaplin.'

Barbara Young

THE MANY-sidedness of Kahlil Gibran is clearly evident throughout all his works. And there are many bits of expression, found and cherished on small pieces of paper, that are like highlights on the tapestry of his story ....

Various opinions of art and poetry were expressed by Gibran in writing at one time or another:

> I believe that the art of today owes its best elements to the Arabs who kept and cherished the spirit in which the Book of the Dead, the Avista, the Book of Job and the Chaldean man-headed winged bull were written and carved. By the art of today I mean that almost religious hunger not yet a century old, which is the golden link between the man of today and the greater man of tomorrow ... The Greek artist had a keener eye and a cleverer hand than the Chaldean or the Egyptian but he did not possess that third Eye which they both possessed. Greece borrowed her gods from Chaldea, Phoenicia and Egypt. She borrowed every quality save that vision, that insight, that peculiar consciousness of what is deeper than depth and higher than height. She brought from Byblos and Nieth the jug and the cup but not the wine. She was capable of fashioning the naively formed jug and cup into golden vessels but she never filled them with aught but liquid realism.
>
> To me the only mighty being in the Greek mythology is Prometheus but let us not forget that the original fire-bringer is Chaldean and not Greek. The races of Western Asia knew him two thousand years before the Trojan expedition.
>
> There are few people in this world who love Greek art as much as I but I love it for what it is, not for what it is not. I love the charm, the freshness, the loveliness, the physical glory of all things Grecian but I cannot find in these the living God. I see only a shadow of His shadow.

A comment on literature:

> The greatest literatures are probably the Arabic or rather the Semitic – for I include the Hebrew – the Greek and the English ... Genius is a protest

against things as they seem to exist. Keats and Shelley were protests. They loved the English scene but they gave it a classic setting in an imaginary world. So did Spenser.

But the Greeks and the Romans were at home with the Greek and the Roman world; they were less like aliens. The French, too, are at home. They accept. Dante did not. He was the greatest of all protests.

And again of Shelley:

He is a world in himself. His soul is that of an excited god, who being sad and weary and homesick, passed the time singing of other worlds. He is in a way the least English of the English poets and the most Oriental from an Oriental point of view.

GIBRAN: THE POET

George Russell (AE)

I DO NOT think the East has spoken with so beautiful a voice since the *Gitanjali* of Rabindranath Tagore as in *The Prophet* of Kahlil Gibran, who is artist as well as poet. Rodin said of him: 'He is the William Blake of the twentieth century'. Two of the drawings are specially moving, one a lovely drooping figure of a girl, the arms outstretched as in crucifixion with the hands nailed to the hearts of two other figures.

I have not seen for years a book more beautiful in thought and when reading it I understand better than ever before what Socrates meant in the *Banquet* when he spoke of the beauty of thought, which exercises a deeper enchantment than the beauty of form. To the mother he cries:

> Your children are not your children,
> They are the sons and daughters of Life's longing for itself.
> You may give them your love but not your thoughts,
> For they have their own thoughts.
> You may house their bodies but not their souls.
> Their souls dwell in the house of to-morrow, which you cannot visit,
>   not even in your dreams.

> He asks of the dweller in the house, has he beauty there –

> Or have you only comfort, that stealthy thing that enters the house a
>   guest and then becomes a host and then a master?

I could quote from every page and from every page I could find some beautiful and liberating thought. How profound is that irony of Gibran's about the lovers of freedom 'who wear their freedom as a yoke and a handcuff'. Have we not seen here souls more chained to their idea of freedom than a prisoner is limited in his cell? The most terrible chains are those that gnaw at the soul. I wonder has the East many more poets to reveal to us? If Europe is to have a new renaissance comparable with that which came from the wedding of Christianity with the Greek and Latin culture it must, I think, come from a second wedding of Christianity with the culture of the East. Our own words to each other bring us no surprise. It is only when a voice comes from India or China or Arabia that we get the thrill of strangeness from the beauty, and we feel that it might inspire another of the great cultural passions of humanity.

Khalil S Hawi

FIRST, HIS doctrine. We have observed that he lived and experienced the ideas which were current in his time, first in Arabic writing and then at the popular level of American thought. The Romantics and Blake had a formative influence on him and this reading of Nietzsche imbued him with an impulse towards power. Therefore we can fairly say that Gibran initiated nothing in the realm of thought, nor did he revive longforgotten ideas. Nevertheless, within these limitations, the pattern of his personal experience has some value of its own. It is no small matter to start life, as he did, with a vision of primitive innocence, to lose it, to know bitterness, alienation from life and despair and then to strive for recovery and rebirth, to succeed in this struggle and to proclaim a reaffirmation of life. For all this he deserves respect. More specifically, we must grant that he attained in *The Prophet* to an optimistic vision of life in which his personal efforts count for more than the influence of popular currents of thought upon him. Not long before this he had said to Mr. Naimy: 'I shall remain bitter so long as there is the taste of bitterness in my mouth'. It is evident from this statement that it was personal experience which guided him more than anything else and therefore this is testimony of his sincerity.

Now, Gibran was speaking as a prophet who believes that his vision is relevant to life and must be able to transform life. How far this was true can be seen from the bearing of his vision on the historical situation of his time and on the civilization of every age. As we shall see presently, his vision failed and was even doomed to failure. His optimistic ideals could not be realized except on the ruins of contemporary civilization, or rather of any and all civilization. Although he called himself a 'lifeist', and insistently praised life in *The Prophet* and elsewhere, civilized life remained incomprehensible to him, nor did he ever try to understand it and reconcile himself to it. His vision was not designed to regenerate the 'old corrupt tree' of *al-'Awāṣif*, which was a symbol of the civilizations of every age. The tree whose root is man and whose flower is God (the symbol used in *The Madman*) was to be a new sapling planted by Gibran in virgin soil. The same tree appears in *The Prophet*.

Also in *The Prophet*, Gibran specifically condemns civilized life during and after bestowing blessings on life. Mrs Young somewhere tells us that he once said: 'I would like to see a modern city without street lights'. In another place she describes his abhorrence of 'the fiery steeds of science' and 'the hell of machinery' and his wish to 'destroy every plane on earth', because he would 'let only the winged spirit of man fly unto the invisible height'. She also tells us that 'he predicted the fall of cities', referring this to a passage in *The Prophet*: '... A little longer shall your city walls separate your hearths from your field'. These remarks recall others in *al-'Awāṣif*, where he says: 'Vain is civilization and vain all that is in it', going on to reject inventions and discoveries as 'playthings by which the mind amuses itself in mood of boredom'.

The prediction of the fall of cities in *The Prophet* is an almost exact repetition of a prophecy made in his adolescence, when he already saw Utopian visions of the future: 'I have seen the city wiped out'. This indicates that the recovery or rebirth of his adult existence was a return to his adolescent ways of thinking, besides being a relapse into primitivism in his view of society. Reinhold Niebuhr has this to say about the rebirth of the spirit in relation to childhood and maturity: 'Spiritual health in both individuals and societies is an achievement of maturity in which some excellence of childhood is consciously reclaimed' and further: 'Romantic primitivism is a false escape from the perils of maturity. A man cannot be a child. A modern nation cannot force itself into the mould of a primitive tribe'.

No doubt the vision Gibran set forth in *The Prophet* shows a noticeable advance from his adolescent vision in the respects of unity and breadth. The book is also richer than anything he had written earlier in touches of revealing insight into small things but the lack of true social and cultural responsibility, which is after all the most important issue, makes it essentially retrogressive and immature. After this how can we take Gibran's assumption of the role of prophet seriously? It becomes merely another proof of his immaturity, primitivism and naivety.

The fact that many people in the United States accepted his mission and that many still do, need not mean that he brought them solutions of their problems or an outlook which was relevant to civilization. We have made it part of our task to interview as many as possible of Gibran's American admirers and followers in Britain and Lebanon and found that most of them were ill adjusted to life and bewildered by its complexities, lacking the strength of nerve and mind either to tolerate or to try to simplify it and that they found a welcome escape route in Gibran's primitivism, disguised, as it is, in the shape of prophecy and oracular wisdom. This furnishes a partial explanation why his works, despite their popularity in the United States, have not been noticed by serious American literary critics and why his name does not appear in books on American literature. We shall give further reasons for this later.

Gibran's early writings about Lebanon did at least show a relative awareness of historical situation and a fresh eye for background and scenery. If he had retained his interest in life in Lebanon or better still, if he had returned to make his home there, this awareness might have deepened over the years. In the United States, on the other hand, he neither participated in the real life of the people nor acquired an imaginative sympathy with their outlook but became a rootless outsider. His personal experience being limited and cut off from the life around him by this failure on his part and by his early primitivism, which eventually soured his outlook on civilized life, his recovery or rebirth was almost inevitably a return to primitivism. Hence his vision was bound to be irrelevant to the situation of his times and the life which he reaffirmed and praised in *The Prophet*, could not be the life of civilized man.

We have dwelt most on Gibran's vision as presented in *The Prophet* because this book is generally considered to be his masterpiece and because it is the work which should justify, if anything could, the role of prophet and teacher which he began to assume early in life, long before he laid open claim to it; the role which is central not only to his thought but also to his literary art and affects the latter in many ways, none of them beneficial in our opinion. For instance, as we have observed before, he preferred to write his narratives in the almost formless form of the romance, rather than that of the modern novel or short story, mainly because this gave him more scope for preaching, commenting on life and the playing of one idea against another. The refined sensibility of the pure poet in him and his gift for language in Arabic enabled him to extend the possibilities his native language held for the expression of subtle tones, colours, shades and emotions and to write lyrical passages of great purity but these gifts were often obscured by the prophet's preference for epigrammatical turns of speech, rhetoric and parables illustrating precepts and morals. So the prophet and teacher with very little that was new to say had overpowered the lyrical poet, obstructed the flow of his song and, what was worse, contaminated him with the vices of the pulpit. In spite of all this, Gibran has his own place in the Arabic literature of his time, first and foremost because he was better qualified than any of his contemporaries to refine the language and introduce the prose poem and next because his advocacy of freedom served to consolidate the tradition of thought which had been initiated by his nineteenth-century predecessors but was not yet firmly enough established.

As to Gibran the poet-prophet who wrote in English, we have evaluated his doctrine and shown that the recognition it won him was of a popular, not a literary kind. We should add that his English style was among the reasons, for this partial failure. First of all, we cannot credit him with a refinement of the English language such as he effected in Arabic, for it had already been refined in the course of its long history by the hands of many poets who were incomparably greater than Gibran. When he came to the use of English, the tide was turning towards a factual language which would make it possible for poetry to deal with the life of the age. Eliot, Pound, the later Yeats and many lesser figures had this aim constantly before them. Gibran's refined language has now to be seen against a background of much greater refinement and against a contemporary trend which makes it look old-fashioned. His open claim to be a prophet had led him to use prophetic forms of expression, the epigram, the aphoristic style and the parable. Needless to say, none of his contemporaries among serious English writers would have regarded these as suitable for modern purposes. Moreover, as a prophet and a rootless outsider whose sensibility had ceased to be nourished by reality, his imagery became more and more general and abstract. Gibran could not challenge the literary world and assert himself in it with this equipment but could only appeal at a popular level to late romantics and seekers after the exotic.

We requested some students of English literature in Cambridge to read Gibran's English works and give us their opinion. This they were kind enough to do and without exception commented that the books were sentimental and poetical, giving those two words the depreciatory sense they have at present. A very few of them showed some interest in *The Madman* because of its ironical tone and lack of sentimentality, but this work is out of print in Great Britain and perhaps in the United States as well, while the millionth copy of *The Prophet* was sold in 1959. This may give some indication of the type of people who admire Gibran in the English-speaking world.

Robert Hillyer

A *Tear and a Smile* includes much of Kahlil Gibran's earliest work, and, with the interesting prose poem written in Paris on his twenty-fifth birthday, marks the beginning of a more mature and affirmative response to life. Like those of many romantic poets, of the East or the West, his youthful flights were toward the white radiance of eternity, away from a world that seemed largely in the hands of injustice and violence. The recoil of a sensitive mind from reality frequently takes revolutionary forms of which political revolution is merely the most obvious. With Gibran the revolt was not directed toward institutions so much as toward the individuals who became the accomplices of abstract evil, of greed, injustice, and bloodshed. Most of the human figures in his early works are therefore personifications, with the result that parable and allegory are the usual method. His later works, more frankly homiletic, gain from the abandonment of the indirect narrative style and present a bolder acceptance of hope for felicity in the here and now.

It is not to be wondered at that in all his works, of whatever period, the teeming memories of his ancient homeland suggest his landscape and metaphors as well as the cast of his thought ....

Lebanon, the native country of Kahlil Gibran, has its full share of such associations. The rites of the ancient church of Antioch are performed within a stone's throw of a ruined temple. The young girls of Christian faith cast flowers into the spring freshets that course down from Mount Lebanon, unaware that they are celebrating the return of Adonis from the realms of death. In 'Before the Throne of Beauty' Gibran pictures Nature as a young girl who is the daughter of the forests. She says to him: 'I am the virgin whom your forefathers did adore; for whom they builded altars and shrines and temples in Baalbek and Aphaca and Byblos'. The poet answers: 'Those temples are destroyed and the bones of my forefathers lie level with the earth and naught remains of their gods and their ways save a few pages between the covers of books'. 'Many of the gods', she tells him, 'live in the life of their adorers and die in their death. Others of them live eternally and forever'. Thus to the young Syrian poet the search for what lives on when the stones fall and the statues crumble led him often to contemplation among the ruins of a civilisation that had collapsed into the debris of others preceding it: the marts, the churches, the fortresses, the Roman temples.

In the portico of such a temple young Gibran observed on his early morning walks a solitary man sitting on the drum of a fallen column and staring into the east. At last he grew bold enough to address the man and ask him what he was doing.

'I am looking at life', was the answer.
'Oh, is that all?'
'Isn't that enough?'

The incident made an impression on Gibran. Somewhere in one of his books he has set it down. I tell it as I remember it from his lips.

The observer of life seated amid the ruins of the past, yet looking toward the coming day; who is alone, unencumbered by the clamour of the city and the collision with other minds: this watcher for the dawn would seem to be Gibran's conception of the poet ....

Gibran's figure of the Poet stands at the top of his hierarchy, far away the highest of mankind. As contemplation of the stars may lift the spirit of some, or the sea the spirit of others, so in Gibran's case the background of his time-scarred country provided a vision of the great and the small, the many and the one, the things that perish and the things that endure, which is the measuring-rod of the poets. Damascus and Lebanon were his earliest memories and from that landscape, similar to the one we imagine in reading the Old Testament, he drew his references. He became an exile; he lived for a time in Paris and finally settled in New York, where he was known to many during the first three decades of the century but he never let go the sinewy hand of his parent country. The unhurried courtesy of the East was in his gestures, her silences and sounds were still with him and at times he spoke with homesick awe of the customs of the church of Syria, against whose orthodoxy he had long since rebelled.

In his youthful revolt against priestcraft he showed a spiritual affinity to the English poet William Blake. As time went on, other aspects of the Occidental mystic's philosophy combined to influence Gibran's writings and his drawings as well. The kinship was clearly discernible and acknowledged. Many convictions were common to both: a hatred of sham and binding orthodoxy, personified by evil priests; the manumission of physical love from the bonds of convention in order to attain spiritual completeness; the perception of beauty in the moment that seems to be fleeting but is, in truth, everlasting; and the discovery of miracles in seasonal nature and the commonplace things of daily living. Both warred against reason in the name of imagination. Both defied the snares of logic to cut a straight path directly to God.

To both Blake and Gibran these revelations are the gift of the poet. The Poet and the Prophet are one. The familiar and majestic lines of Blake express the bardic ideal:

> Hear the voice of the Bard,
> Who present, past and future sees;
> Whose ears have heard

The Holy Word
That walk'd among the ancient trees ....

And in this present volume we read these lines from 'A Poet's Voice':

> Say of me what you will and the morrow will judge you, and your words shall be a witness before its judging and a testimony before its justice .... I came to say a word and I shall utter it. Should death take me ere I give voice, the morrow shall utter it .... That which alone I do today shall be proclaimed before the people in days to come.

In Gibran's *Prophet* a separate character is assigned to the Poet, yet they are two aspects of the same entity, the highest emanation of Man. The poet can sin only in denying his own nature – and in all Gibran's pages no poet commits such a sin. Even in conversation with friends Gibran maintained the same high seriousness toward what was to him a sacred office. I remember one afternoon over thirty years ago in Gibran's studio. Young and easily embarrassed, I had let fall an evasive and perhaps frivolous remark in response to a characterisation of me as a young poet. It was trifling; I have forgotten it. But I have not forgotten how Gibran looked at me long and intently as if searching out my real nature, and at last made some observation on the sacredness of poetry and the high calling of its votaries, which disposed of any possibility of touching the subject lightly. 'Ah', he concluded, 'but you must not talk that way, you must not do the usual things that other men do, for a poet is holy'. A lifetime passion was behind the quiet rebuke ....

In *Nymphs of the Valley* we read the story of the poor boy tormented by the wicked monks; in *Spirits Rebellious* it is the Priest who pronounces the curse over the bodies of the bride and her lover who died faithful to their love.

We of the West cannot weigh the factual truth of Gibran's portrayal of the priesthood in his youthful works. It may be that the Syrian Church of his boyhood was indeed the purveyor of corruption, the jewelled bauble empty of significance, the oppressor of the poor, as he describes it. Remnants of Byzantine splendour along with Byzantine decay may cling to the Eastern churches: the poet's indignation cannot be wholly without reference to observed conditions. The Eastern churches have never undergone the purgation by heresy and reformation that has cleansed the Western churches.

Yet it must be remembered that the Oriental method of personifying institutions and summoning an entire situation into one symbol was characteristic of Gibran's work, especially in his novitiate as poet. Truth to a large design, as in Byzantine art, sometimes demanded the distortion of details. His realism consisted in the massing of general effects to emphasise concepts that he believed to be the ultimate reality. Thus he was at the opposite pole from contemporary realists who overwhelm large themes in an avalanche of careful detail. In this fact lies much of Gibran's appeal for the reader who wearies of the modern Occidental technique, which so often leads to the gutter and away from the stars. The photographic reproduction of actuality with no reference to the more expansive designs of Truth and Justice, Beauty and Peace, would have held no interest for Gibran ....

In spite of the impressiveness of the conclusion, we are aware that the symbolic method in such a story is far too generalised to support the scrutiny of truth. It becomes little more than sentimentalism, gilded by the rays of uncertain artistry. Sentimentalism of this kind is the prevailing weakness of young romantics, including, at times, the young Blake.

With the Poor Man and the Poet, the Lover completes the trinity of noble personages. In the early parables physical union, but delicately hinted at, is the consummation, the release of the soul. There is no sustained emphasis on the sensualism we associate with the love poetry of the Orient, and even the discernible echoes from the *Song of Songs* are chastened and become rather remote. In 'The Tale of a Friend' we are told that 'love comes in many guises. Sometimes it is as wisdom, other times justice, oft-times hope. My love for him was my hope that the strong light of its sun might triumph over the darkness of transient sorrows. But I knew not when and where filthiness became a clean thing, and cruelty kindness and ignorance wisdom. A man knows not in what manner the spirit is freed from matter until after it is freed'. ...

Evidently Gibran left behind him very early his childhood conception of individual redemption and survival as taught in Christianity. In the theory of reincarnation of the soul the identity half persists through a succession of new experiences with no recollection of what has gone before except in occasional flashes of revelation. At last he surrendered his last vestige of belief in the survival of the individual and spoke of the reunion of that particle of deity, that small kingdom of God within each man, with the all-embracing Godhead. The rest is the dross of this world, gratefully to be relinquished as the soul takes its lonely flight back to its Source.

A Tear and a Smile exhibits this somewhat emotional philosophy at its most untamed. If the parables and observations lack the serenity of *The Prophet* or *The Madman*, they have some compensating vigour, almost a rashness, of approach, natural to a young writer who, had he been born in the West, would have been a late recruit to the romantic school. The book is more Eastern, however, than his later writings. It is probable that in these Arabic compositions he was writing for his countrymen at home and in exile. That is a larger audience than many are aware of and international in scope ....

The contrast here between the Northern and Eastern mysticism is worth mentioning.

Gibran's strength developed not from a change of technique but from a change in emphasis. It would be unnatural for a mature poet to continue to express nothing but loathing for the world in which he lives and always to point 'yonder'. Such grimly maintained irony in English and American poetry of the past generation has resulted in a wasteland of lamentations which, on analysis, prove to be but the vulgar exposure of personal woes and inadequacies. The phrasing is tough, but the core is effeminate. Poetry cannot proceed along a series of negations. Gibran's best work, embellished though it is with Asian metaphor, develops manlier qualities. Hope, cheerfulness and anger displace the perhaps overworked tears and smiles, and they increase as the poet grows older.

The second half of the present volume is in the main given over to these more positive moods. 'The Widow and her Son' is a dignified little *genre* piece wherein the treasure of the humble is adequately realised. Patriotism is in the inspiration of 'A People and Destiny', wherein Syria, personified as a shepherdess, consults with Destiny, in the guise of an old man, with something keener than mere wistfulness for a vanished past. 'Behold the sun rising from out of darkness' – the conclusion of 'Peace' – becomes gradually the prevailing theme. The Sun, moreover, is not only that eventual and spiritual orb to be reached through the gates of suffering and death, but the good daily sun, warming the earth to a genial response, a felicity in the here and now, an assurance of terrestrial bliss.

Thus in his first flights the poet sped toward eternity and saw the world as a place where misfortune must purify the soul for its reunion with God. Then the increasing warmth of life led him to be less dualistic: the material world became informed with the heavenly light. Gibran's ripened philosophy is anticipated in several of the selections here, prominently in 'My Birthday', written in Paris when he became twenty-five. In this piece he explicitly turns away from his past writings and drawings in the sudden arrival of a joy he had not imagined: a meaning in the faces of people, their voices rising upward in the streets of the city, children at play, young men and old, and so beyond that city, not in escape but in understanding, to 'the wild parts in their awful beauty and voiced silence', then on to the sea, the stars and 'all the contending ... forces of attraction and repulsion ... created and borne by that Will, timeless and without limit'. We are reminded of the climax of Victor Hugo's famous 'Extase':

> Et les étoiles d'or, légions infinies,
> A voix haute à voix basse, avec mille harmonies,
> Disaient, en inclinant leurs couronnes de feu;
> Et les flots bleus, que rien ne gouverne et n'arrête,
> Disaient, en recourbant l'écume de leur crête:
> – C'est le Seigneur, le Seigneur Dieu!

At the end Gibran discovers and acknowledges that 'humanity is the spirit of divineness on earth', and 'what I now say with one tongue, tomorrow will say with many'.

The poet grows up. The detestable Priests and Rich Men disappear; the impeccable Poets and Lovers take on more lively attributes than mere flawlessness. Eternity becomes more than a distant star wherein we shall quench the small, wandering fire of our being. It begins to shine through the earth, not away from it.

Beauty itself must take on earthly form if it is to summon humanity toward its own perfection. As Gibran says in one of the finest pieces in this book, 'The Child Jesus': 'My life was a tale of woe; now it is become a joyful thing. And it will be turned to bliss, for the arms of the Child have enfolded my heart and embraced my soul'.

Mikhail Naimy

I N THE creative life of every man of genius there is always a certain peak which, once attained, he can never surpass. Slowly, laboriously and often unconsciously he traces his path to that peak. Only when at the top can he look down and bless every step in his upward climb even though drenched in his heart's blood. He is not aware, however, that the moment he leaves that peak he is no longer destined to rise to a taller one beyond it. One the contrary, he may slip many furlongs below it.

Rare indeed are the men of exceptional gifts who have reached in their particular field two or more peaks of equal height and splendour. Perhaps Shakespeare may be cited as one of those exceptions. For one is at a loss to choose between such peaks as *Hamlet*, *King Lear* and *Macbeth* and say which is the highest. They all seem dazzlingly lofty and brilliant. Whereas you can easily pick this work or that of most toilers in the various fields of human endeavour and declare it as their very best.

In the case of Gibran one can assert without the slightest hesitation that his book *The Prophet* represents the peak in his literary career. Viewed in the light of Reincarnation, a doctrine which he embraced and made the cornerstone of his philosophy of human destiny, Gibran's life from his own birth to the birth of *The Prophet* may be seen as a steady ascent to that peak. It was not by blind chance that he was born on the brink of a deep and most gorgeous valley in Northern Lebanon known as the Holy Valley, or the Valley of Saints (Wadi Qadisha) and within a stone's throw of the famous cedar grove nestling in the shade of Cedar Mountain which towers more than 9000 feet above the Mediterranean. That grove, with a patriarch cedar whose age is a mere score of centuries, represents the straggling remnants of a once mighty forest that covered almost all of the mountains of Lebanon. Nor was any step Gibran took an accidental step, from the moment he began to toddle and up to the moment he breathed his last at Saint Vincent's hospital in the city of New York.

Without going into the details of Gibran's life I can safely say that in his estimation and mine, all his pre-*Prophet* works, whether in Arabic or in English, were but so many stages in his ascent towards the ultimate peak. Beginning with *Music*, his earliest attempt in Arabic, and passing through *The Prairie Nymphs* [*Nymphs of the Valley*], *Spirits*

Rebellious, *A Tear and a Smile*, *The Broken Wings*, *The Processions*, *The Tempests* – all in Arabic – and *The Madman* and *The Forerunner* – in English – one is made instantly aware that one is face to face with an extremely sensitive soul groping its way towards a goal whose contours are yet wrapped in mist.

Only an equally sensitive soul can imagine what Gibran's soul experienced in its upward march towards the cherished peak. Because that peak was still in the distance and enveloped in a thick veil of haze and because Gibran was not yet certain of his path, it was natural that he should find himself ill at ease in a world engrossed in all varieties of passions except the passion to achieve the great and the glorious. Even in his early life Gibran abhorred the commonplace and the ordinary. The greatness and the glory he dreamt of was the greatness and glory of a Shakespeare, a Keats, a Michelangelo, a da Vinci.

Not only did Gibran detest the ordinary and the trivial; it tortured him to see so much hypocrisy in religion and so much arrogance in the topmost circles of the church hierarchy. It pained him no less to see temporal authority strut with so much pomp, and browbeat the ones who happened to be low in the social scale. Equally painful to him was the total disregard of justice in the distribution of human fortunes. Particularly depressed was he by the lot of Woman in a society ruled by Man. Therefore his early outpourings breathed at times a melancholy bordering on despair; at other times they were volcanic lava meant to engulf all the hypocrites and despots, and all the social orders and systems that defiled the divine in Man. Now and then he would lull his turbulent and anguished soul by sweet, romantic musings.

At one time Gibran thought he had found himself and his path. It was when he fell on Nietzsche's *Thus Spoke Zarathustra*. That book swept him off his feet. Its bitter and sweeping denunciation of all human values except what it called the Superman seemed to give vent to Gibran's own pent-up hostility to all existing human beliefs and conventions. In 'The Grave-Digger' his greatest joy and his sole preoccupation become the digging of graves for all the living since they have long been dead, although they knew it not. The same vein is carried further in such books as *The Madman* and *The Forerunner*, although much less in the latter than in the former.

Perhaps the most delightful piece in *The Madman* is the one entitled 'The Perfect World'. Never have I read a more bitter, more sarcastic upbraiding of the smug American world in particular, and the human world in general, where everything is 'cut to order' as it were. Such a world would appear suffocating to a man like Gibran, whose gaze is set on something quite different, but as yet not very clear. The mist had not yet lifted, and the outlines of the peak were still hazy. But this also was a necessary step in the ascent. Gibran had to chafe, mock and flail, if for no other reason than to ease his tormented soul and to remove what he considered as so much debris on his way to a goal not yet clear and definite.

It was during that period of storm and stress in Gibran's life that he spoke so often and so much not of his loneliness but of his *aloneness*, as if he were fighting a battle against the whole world, and all by himself. Friedrich Nietzsche who had fought such a battle before, finished his fight in an insane asylum and was no longer among the living. Will he, the stranger in a strange world, the obscure boy born in an obscure village at the foot of Cedar Mountain in distant Lebanon, be able to carry the battle alone and in the face of such tremendous odds?

Whether because he came to realize that the task was entirely beyond his power; or whether because some forces dormant in his deeper being began to stir and to rebel against the rebellious grave-digger who had taken such a hold on his soul, Gibran, almost unconsciously, began to regain his temporarily lost Eastern self, – that self brought up on the divine milk and bread of 'The Nazarene' and on the teachings of those who had introduced to the world the revolutionary idea of Reincarnation and all the intricate laws of retribution that flow from it. From time to time flashes like those of lightning began to pierce the murky atmosphere enveloping his restless spirit. As if coming home after a protracted and arduous trip in foreign lands, that spirit was no longer busy digging graves for all living men and women. On the contrary, it was most ready and anxious to fraternize with them, from the lowest to the highest. In fact it no longer classified them as high and low, clean or unclean, worthy or unworthy. It no longer sat in judgment over them. It came to see its own clay no whit nobler than their clay. It was ready not only to condone their sins, but accept them as its own.

The rebel against all established human orders came to realize that those orders were but so many small details in a much vaster and much more grandiose scheme which may be called the Cosmic Order or the Cosmic Scheme. The wheel turning to the right amid a host of wheels all turning to the left (the words are Gibran's) suddenly found that in reality it was turning in perfect harmony with the rest of the wheels in the fantastically huge and complicated machine of the infinite Universe, in which the human element is but a drop in the ocean. Thus the mist beclouding his vision as he made his ascent began to disperse and the peak was not only within sight, but also within reach, splendid and clearly etched against the sky.

It was during 1922, when I was with him at his studio, that Gibran read me the sermon on Love with which Almustafa opens his series of sermons to the people of Orphalese. It was in that same studio that he read me, from time to time, all the subsequent sermons. Shortly before *The Prophet* came out in 1923 Gibran handed me a typescript of it, which I cherish to this day as one of the most precious souvenirs he left me. No less precious is the printed copy of the first edition of the book which bears his inscription in Arabic 'To my beloved brother and companion Mikhail'. In those days I could easily read in Gibran's face and hear in his voice the joyous relaxation of a mountain climber who had reached the summit. Down deep in his heart he fully realized that every step he had taken on his way to that summit could not have been vain or superfluous. It was a necessary link in a long chain.

Inscrutable, indeed, are the ways of Fortune. Having reached his peak Gibran thought it within him to reach still higher ones. He spoke to me of his intention to write two sequels to *The Prophet* which would make of it a trilogy: *The Prophet*, *The Garden of the Prophet* and *The Death of the Prophet*. That trilogy was not destined to see the light. What was published after Gibran's death as *The Garden of the Prophet* was an abortive connection of one or two pieces written by Gibran for that purpose with the rest of the pages of that most slender book filled with translations of some Arabic pieces written by Gibran long before *The Prophet* and with some brazen insertions by a pen other than Gibran's. As for the other books that followed *The Prophet*, such as *Sand and Foam*, *Jesus: The Son of Man*, *The Earth Gods* and the posthumous *Wanderer*, they all fall short of the peak. 'In this country and this age,

Mischa', Gibran once said to me when he brought out *Sand and Foam*, 'one must keep abreast. Else one is likely to be soon forgotten. We must remind the readers of ourselves from time to time'.

Others will speak to you at this festival, and at some length, of Gibran's *Prophet* and other books. They will also speak to you of Gibran the artist and of the other sides of his rich and many-sided life. My purpose is to give merely a hint of what he has found and experienced at his peak.

Once on the peak, Gibran casts a backward glance at the trail he has trudged with so much anguish and pain from the base of the mountain to the top. His heart is now full of affection for all things and beings whom he once denounced as stumbling-blocks and who appear to him now as so many stepping-stones to the peak. He realizes that the peak on which he stands is not his ultimate goal. Away in the distance and bathed in shimmering light, looms the picture of his 'isle of birth', his divine homeland where everything is peace, love and beauty undying. To reach that land he must, and not 'without a pain in the spirit', tear himself away from places and faces which had become extremely dear to his heart. His words of farewell to them are so warm, so sweet and so touching that hearing or reading them one is made aware of the tremendous power of love when it springs from the deepest depths of a heart-cleansed of all animosity, distrust, suspicion and the 'holier than thou' attitude towards other human hearts.

With that love as his spring-board, Almustafa plunges himself and his hearers into a state of consciousness wherein all men are made to share in one another's sins and virtues, and are taught to refrain from judging one another. 'And if any of you', says Almustafa, 'would punish in the name of righteousness and lay the axe unto the evil tree, let him see to its roots; and verily he will find the roots of the good and the bad, the fruitful and the fruitless, all entwined together in the silent heart of the earth'. How reminiscent are these words of Christ's words: 'Whoever of you is without sin let him cast the first stone'.

Again and again does Almustafa remind the people of Orphalese of what he calls their 'God-self'. Too prone are they to be carried away by their pigmy human self perpetually wriggling in a huge cobweb of laws, traditions and conventions all catering to the flesh and entirely oblivious of their nobler origin and their higher aspirations for freedom from fetters of all kinds. It is only when they discover their giant self, – the God within them, – that they will taste the true joy of living. Love, charity, compassion, forgiveness, taming of the proud and misguided ego, – all these and others of the same quarry are luminous milestones on the way to discovery of the God-self.

In conclusion I must say that one will not do justice to a book like *The Prophet* if one is to take it as a book of instructions only. Its greater value, in my judgment, lies in the mould in which those instructions are cast. Because he was a consummate artist, Gibran was able to make his Almustafa sing sweet melodies and paint exquisite pictures as he expounded his views of human life to the people of Orphalese. Those songs and those pictures have something intoxicating in them. Never before or after had Gibran attained that mastery of sound and colour. Therefore will *The Prophet* remain the highest and noblest peak of Gibran's comparatively short but very rich life.

To honour such a book and its author is, in truth, to honour ourselves and the country that gave them birth. Such books and such men are our surety that Humanity, despite the fearful dissipation of its incalculable energies and resources, is not yet bankrupt.

May the light of the beacon Gibran set on high never be dimmed!

Francis Warner

If, in this ancient land of soaring hills
And spreading cedars, I have food for tears,
It is perhaps that nowhere else so fills
The traveller's heart with ease from all his cares.
For we have walked with you your winding streets,
Seen the sun high on liveliness, I know;
Yet throughout all a natural blessing greets
With childhood promise everywhere I go.
Your valleys, waterfalls and snowy heights,
Your Song of Songs, your sadness and your joys
Bring me strange intuitions that such sights
Will strengthen life, wherever grief destroys.
   And I believe, when hope's flame gutters low
   Bisharri shows us truths that make it grow.

Aïcha Lemsine Laïdi

K AHLIL GIBRAN will surely have in the centuries to come more eloquent interpreters than me ... but the recognition of what the women writers of my generation owe to him is too precious to leave it to silence.

As an Algerian author raised with two languages I find myself in Kahlil Gibran's linguistic plurality. This Master has been one of the pioneers of the revival of Arabic, the language of the Koran, and has given to English the spiritual and sensual inspiration of the Orient.

But Kahlil Gibran is overall this unique voice trying to find itself in the bubbling and the diversity of the thought; this voice which proclaimed that 'Art is the only means to God beyond the human condition'.

To this brother from Lebanon, altogether poet, philosopher, painter, and mystic, we are indebted for a teaching full of high examples of virtue and human wisdom far from complacency and fanaticism. A stirring teaching, vivid and flexible as only can be the soul of a poet ... or a prophet.

How many precious jewels of humanity one can find in his maxims in *Sand and Foam* ... where the heart and the spirit join together in the beauty of these words: 'Neither a master nor a slave' – and in this humble prayer: 'God let me be the lion's prey before having the rabbit as my prey'.

And yet whatever numerous the works of a writer could be, it seems that the very roots of thought and the art of an author lie in one particular masterpiece, as it appears for example with Shakespeare and *Hamlet* or James Joyce and *Ulysses* ... in the likeness of Kahlil Gibran who will remain forever inseparable from *The Prophet*. This book about which Kahlil Gibran himself said: 'I was born to live and to write one book'.

In this respect I make bold to say that *The Prophet* was created only thanks to the revolt of *Spirits Rebellious*; that first book burnt by the invaders and the clergymen ... this prime work burnt at the stake of intolerance has been the assured itinerary in the quest of 'silences'....

This is to say that for Arab women and for those all over the world who fight against iniquity and violence, Kahlil Gibran is also the just rebel, a magnificent example of a conscience striving to rise towards God.

However Kahlil Gibran is not the prophet of God, but that of Man. He is our word beside God. The word of our word as it appears in one of his excerpts:

> The first thought of God was an angel
> His first word was Man.

Kathleen Raine

THE END of the nineteenth century might be seen as the final triumph of rational materialism based on natural science as the accepted orthodoxy of the Western and Westernized world; yet in retrospect can we not see that whereas materialist civilization (whether Marxist or capitalist) was in its terminal phase, a powerful counter-current was flowing – not through one mind only but as if some collective spiritual power found agents where it could. In India there were holy men equal to any teachers of her golden age – Ramakrishna, Vivekananda, Ramana, Maharshi, Sri Aurobindo, and Mahatma Gandhi's inspired faith in the power of non-violence to change the world; Yeats's friend AE's vision of a world where 'the politics of time' would be conducted according to the 'politics of eternity'; Yeats himself who totally rejected the materialism of his time and scanned the whole horizon of his world for a learning of the Imagination through which wisdom and poetry might return. Gibran, re-visioning Christianity in the light of Islamic (Sufi) mysticism, is of this group of inspired teachers of the modern world. All these were persecuted in one way or another: Gandhi was repeatedly imprisoned. Yeats himself, great world-poet as he was, was ridiculed by his contemporaries who were ignorant of the great mainstream of civilization from which he drew his knowledge. Gibran was dismissed for the opposite reason, because of his immense following of ordinary men and women, for he answered to a deep need within the Western world, starved as it was of its spiritual food. Communism and capitalism alike have believed that mankind could be fed on 'bread alone' but once again the prophets of the ever-living spirit have shown that the 'Word of God' is the necessary food of the soul. It is as if one mind had spoken through several voices, none more eloquent or beautiful than the lonely voice of the Christian Lebanese Arab, Kahlil Gibran.

GIBRAN: THE ARTIST

Yusuf Huwayyik

NOW WHEN I close my eyes, how quickly the memory of Gibran comes to my mind – his affectionate smile, warm voice and expressive hands. I can see us walking to the Luxembourg Garden, turning left and sitting on the roof which overlooks the Palace and a part of the garden. I can hear the echo of Gibran's voice in my year, 'We are in Paris, Yusuf! In this rich garden and on this road stretching before us walked many great learned men and artists. I can feel the presence of Puvis de Chavannes, Carrière, Balzac, Alfred de Musset, Victor Hugo, Pasteur, Curie, Taine and Renan. I feel as if I can trace their footprints on this road'.

Alice Raphael

THE LIVES of former generations are a lesson to posterity.' This quotation from the volume which is currently accepted as the masterpiece of ancient Arabic literature, *The Thousand and One Nights*, serves in a slightly paraphrased form as a fitting introduction to the work of the most authoritative artist and poet of modern Arabia – Kahlil Gibran.

In the near East, there are over a hundred million whose native language is Arabic and the poetry of Gibran has become so incorporated with the national traditions of these people that one is not quoting lightly in saying that 'the works of the present generation are a lesson to posterity'. But Gibran the poet, who has been known to the Arabian world of letters as poet, critic and historian for twenty-four years, has already been introduced to the English reading public by his book *The Madman*, a collection of poems and parables, some translated by him for his own works in Arabic and others written directly in English with an admirable fluency and command of the Western tongue.

It is Gibran the painter whose drawings are now being brought to the attention of his American audience and the following interpretation of his art will perhaps serve as a clue to the ever entrancing mystery of the harmonies and dissonances which exist between the East and the West.

Kahlil Gibran was born in Mt. Lebanon and although he has deliberately chosen to identify himself with the new world and its surging problems, his affiliations with Syria form such a vital part of his life that in this instance it seems as if the links between the old world and the new were admirably forged and adequately tempered. Despite the fact that he feels himself to be essentially a Syrian and that he is acclaimed as the authoritative spokesman for the Arabic people in the allied arts, Gibran belongs to the world outside nationalistic interests and his art is a product of a deep sympathy with the problems which constitute the moving current of life in all nations and throughout all ages. His poetry is a blend of ancient imagery coupled with the poignant irony of modern introspection, and his painting is also a product of the abundant fantasies of the Orient set forth with as scrupulous a perfection of technique as the West has ever produced.

It is this blend of the poet and the painter which makes his work stand apart from the modern poetry of the East which we have come to know in the work of Tagore for instance, and which separates his painting from the traditional concept of Oriental art. For Gibran, in spite of his filial allegiance to Syria, is a citizen of the land of Cosmopolis – that ever moving realm, somewhat like the fabled island of Atlantis, which belongs to all times and to no particular place; so that Gibran, besides being the most widely read poet of modern Arabia, is also closely affiliated with Paris. There he worked with Rodin and he exhibited at the Salon a series of portraits, which included Debussy,

Rostand, Sarah Bernhardt, and Rodin himself, who said: 'I know of no one else in whom drawing and poetry are so linked together as to make him a new Blake'.

His sensitive appreciation of the interrelation of the arts enables him to be the spokesman for the genius of the Arabic people to whom the Western world owes a debt which it is only beginning now to appreciate and no poet of former generations has done more to bring about a closer understanding between the East and the West than Kahlil Gibran.

Tagore, for instance, belongs exclusively to India. Whether we read him or not – whether we incorporate his work with that of other modern schools, nevertheless this does not affect the value of Tagore to India. For he has not lived in the land of Cosmopolis nor does he lend his interests to the new era in Western literature. But Gibran has chosen to co-operate with Western arts and letters and his faith in the development of our 'static culture' is indeed a lesson to posterity.

He has surrendered his position as a leader in the world of the Near East in order to bring the traditions and genius of the Arabic people to the attention of the Western world. And although commentators have long since acknowledged our debt in literature to the Arabs, who introduced rhyme into Europe over a thousand years ago, and historians have admitted the impetus which was given to the sciences by Arabic philosophers, yet it remains the task of a modern to introduce us in painting to the vast poetical conceptions which constitute a part of the heritage of the Arabian race mind.

Kahlil Gibran is one of the artists who are engaged in the struggle between the old and the new, or as in other times, the conflict was termed, the oscillation between the classic and the romantic tendencies in art. As a poet, he is a Romanticist, moving abreast the times and incorporating the keenly analytic spirit of our age into the ancient parable or the simple form of rhythmic prose. But in painting he is a Classicist and his work owes more to the findings of da Vinci than it does to any of our modern insurgents. Thus Gibran is also caught in the struggle which is the besetting problem of the world today, the reconstruction of an era which will adjust the imperishable legacy of the old world, the classic traditions, with the ever evolving, fluctuating tendencies in art which constitute the essence of true Romanticism.

For the cataclysm which has overwhelmed our world and is causing us to reconstruct our geographical boundaries and political tenets, also demands us to reconstruct our moral valuations and our standards in the life of the soul, of which art is one of the most profound manifestations. And as we think back upon the destruction which has separated the world with which we were familiar from the world in which we move today, we become more and more aware of the cataclysm which has so completely shattered our philosophies, dogmas and artistic beliefs.

A sombre burden has descended upon the shoulders of the coming generation, whose task it is to create a world as yet in embryo – and if our arts are not to go down before such inspirations as the camouflage, and if science is not to be prostituted to such creations as the tank – if a nobler expression of energy is yet to redeem man from the pit into which his destructive power has plunged him, then in the period of reconstruction he must insensibly turn to new and more vital forms of self-expression. Religion in the traditional meaning can no longer lift him out of the rut of his suffering and only in another form of expression which will portray the realities of the soul devoutly, either in terms of art, science or social creeds, will he be able to effect a transition between the death agony of the old world and the travail of the new.

But even in this dark traverse though which we are passing in an effort to win a new life as our own, we are aware of certain germinating influences which already foreshadow the art of the future, so that the productions of an artist can never be evaluated in terms of self-expression alone but must be measured by their relation to the organic processes of which they are an integral part.

To the interpretive mind, for instance, the destruction of Carthage cannot be judged as a pyrotechnical display of military prowess, for that which is significant was the impetus of change which that act gave to civilization. With the import of the cult of Cybele, the great Mother, Rome was placed in direct communication with the East and a contact between the modern and the ancient world was firmly established. Eventually, the religion and the art of the East not only acquired a foothold, but became an integral part of later Roman culture, so that Rome was conquered by that which centuries before it had set out to subdue. The Romans set out to conquer a rival and brought back the religion and thereby much of their rival's system of power. In this way a process which on the surface was nationalistic became fundamentally a part of the organic evolution of civilization, which redirected the cultural processes of a nation and eventually of what was, then, the modern world.

Thus the term 'modern' loses its coin value when we see how lightly it can be shifted from era to era, denoting certain types of ideas rather than periods of time. For the life of the inner world is without boundaries other than personal limitations, without national or particularistic interests other than those we voluntarily adopt. We shift our emotional contents upon a word like 'Spartacide' and it becomes a modern equivalent; it is at once cut adrift from its original connotation and it becomes vitally related to our own interests and feelings. In short the word, the symbol, flashes the past to life and passes on meaning into the present in order to stimulate the mind to seek out new intellectual pastures.

For the soul is occupied with but a few problems and these are singularly few. Life in its elemental functioning is but a transformation of the processes of Birth, Love and Death. The hunger of the appetites and the hunger of possession; the desire for adventure and the fear of the unknown; to love and to be loved; out of these essential simplicities, man has erected the vast complexities of life and to these essential simplicities the artist must return who seeks a new means of expression amidst the clutter of religions, arts and moralities.

Those who have witnessed the disintegration of a world can no longer find satisfaction in objective painting. What has the art of Messonier to say to a man who has lived in a trench? What has the art of Watteau to offer to men who have experienced shrapnel or the submarine? We know that Veronese worked amidst the voluptuous realities which he depicted; we know that Watteau fantasised the shepherd and shepherdess exquisitely, but to us this type of painting is merely interesting because of its historic value. Intrinsically, it has no message to offer us.

It is at this point in art that symbolism reveals itself as the interrelating principle between the life of the soul and objective life; that is to say that just as the symbol of the word is the interchanging coin between ancient and modern concepts, so in art, the symbolic meaning is the interchanging medium between the modern and the antique. Yet before we apply the word 'symbolic' to an artist we must first come to a clear concept of its value, for it is a word which one approaches with hesitancy as its meaning has become so clouded by misuse that our mind flashes instantly to that group who were thus classified and then to the satirical lyric of the man 'walking down Piccadilly with a lily in his mediaeval hand'.

We can get no clearer picture of symbolism in art than by recalling that period and school which gave every appearance of it and yet never possessed its essence. The pre-Raphaelites, for instance, attempted to recreate in their mode and manner, that which was for ever past just as certain modernists attempt a crude simplicity which was only characteristic of primitive humanity. The true symbolist is concerned with the life of the inner world. To his eyes the changing cultures of man are merely transformations upon which he focuses his attention. Whereas, to the ideationist – the objective artist – each epoch, each stratum in the history of man is a separate and distinct reality and he occupies himself depicting the surfaces and planes of the outer expression of life. He is in constant relation to the present; he has no personal affiliation with the vast spiritual life of the past and possesses no embryonic concept of the future.

But to the true symbolist life is a perpetual recreation and he moves in a world freed from traditions and confines. He need not attempt to escape from the limitations of the present by seeking the mannerisms of an enigmatic past. He is in direct contact with that past and hence the future is an ever fluid and ever luminous atmosphere; he is at one with fundamentals.

If we examine the work of the early Primitives we see at once how deeply imbued they were with the essence of symbolism. In fact, they cared so deeply for the spirit of the idea that the manner of its presentation caused them little concern. They covered the walls of Assisi because they wished to tell the story of Jesus that others might know and profit by it. To them, Jesus was a reality, not a story about which to make a painting, and consequently it was a matter of difference to Ghirlandaio whether the women attending the Virgin wore the dresses of his own age or those of antiquity. They were the women attending the Virgin and that which has given the Santa Maria Novella its lustre, is the power of a feeling, visioned, experienced, grasped – and then put forth again.

However, in the minds of the pre-Raphaelites, the vision was most assiduously cultivated. Their very pre-occupation proves them to have been objective artists diverted from their proper functioning. They did not seek the vision of England, which would have been their true expression, the sentimental Victorian England of their day, but they turned their eyes towards the Italy of the past and became blinded by the dust of the centuries which lay upon it. The result was narrative art, a beautiful and ingenious affectation of the source of inspiration, but the symbols of love and sorrow, of joy and pain became involved in confused mysticism. For the pre-Raphaelites sought not their own spirit but that of another, not the meaning within but that lying as far away as possible – in fact the more remote it was, the more they sought it. They reproduced instead of creating, and they have given us beautiful stories, beautiful pictures, beautiful ideas – everything except that which can never be reproduced, and that is the spirit of their own age.

In the separation of the symbolist from the ideationist, the art of the East is most concisely divided from the art of the West. To the East the lotus is a flower, but also a symbol of divinity; to the West it is a flower developing into the acanthus design and completing the circle, it becomes a decoration, and so again only a flower. Again the earth, the sun, the sea, that which is above, and that which lies beneath, are to the Western mind, materials of study to be touched, represented, understood and grasped. But to the East, it suffices that these things are and will be eternally, and that behind these realities which we visualize and know, lie other and again other forces and experiences, other suns, other seas, melting mysteriously into one another as the leaves of the lotus.

It is at this dividing line of East and West, of the symbolist and the ideationist, that the work of Kahlil Gibran presents itself as an arresting type in our concept of painting. He has accepted both the traditions of form and the inner meaning of the idea, and he exhibits both a new type of work and another method of approach to fundamental truths.

The qualities of the East and the West are blended in him with a singular felicity of expression, so that while he is the symbolist in the true sense of the word, he is not affixed to traditional expression, as he would be if he were creating in the manner of the East, and though he narrates a story as definitely as any pre-Raphaelite, it is without any fanfare of historical circumstances nor any of the accompaniment of symbolic accessories. In his art there is no conflict between whether the idea shall prevail over the emotion, or whether emotion shall sway the thought, because both are so equally established that we are not conscious of one or the other as dominant. They co-exist in harmony and the result is an expression of sheer beauty in which thought and feeling are equally blended. In this fusion of two opposing tendencies the art of Gibran transcends the conflicts of schools and is beyond the fixed conceptions of the classic or romantic traditions.

An illuminating beauty informs his work; to him the idea becomes beautiful if it is true; the emotion becomes truth if it is real. He possesses a singular power of dividing what is essential from what is extraneous in the presentation of beauty and truth. And he keeps to a simplicity of manner in the portrayal of an idea which is closely akin to the spirit of the Primitives, albeit the art of the centuries has gone into the moulding of his powers; but in his statements he is simple, almost instinctively simple. In fact, he may be described as an intuitive artist – as that type of artist whose feeling is like the divining rod which leads down to shafts of golden values and who does not obfuscate his mind with intellectual concepts of what or how he should create. And having followed his instinctive flair for truth he now applies his conscious powers to perfect his finding and to create his embryonic expressions into paintings of beauty and value.

He needs only a small sheet of paper to give us the meaning of the 'Erdgeist'; we see the body of a woman who rises out of the vast form of the All-Mother, carrying in her arms man and woman. Only the head of the unfolding mother with its mysterious smile is drawn in what we are accustomed to think of as drawing. There is the story, interpret it as you will; Erda – Amida – Ceres – Mary – the choice is a matter of time and temperament. The meaning is the same and Gibran is dealing with fundamentals.

But in the portrayal of the idea he is scrupulously faithful to the perfection of his technique. Thus, beauty is the final arbiter upon the destiny of his production. He creates with intuitive feeling then shapes his work into unity with the power of thought, but both these impulses are guided and guarded by a profound love and appreciation of the beautiful which enables him to portray that which he has to say as simply and as sincerely as it is possible for him to do. It is this quality of instinctive simplicity which makes his painting so clearly akin to the art of the sculpture, for the sculptor, unless in relief, cannot deal with anything other than the essential idea and the beauty of form. In sculpture there are no accessories of background, no gradations of colour values to attract the eye and deflect the mind from thought. Very few painters have been able to express the essentials of life in painting. Da Vinci attempted it but he was lured away from the quest by his love of subtleties, and pupils like Luini or Sodoma expressed the subtleties but failed to grasp the inner meaning which held da Vinci to his perpetual quest.

The art of Gibran is symbolic in the deepest meaning of the word because its roots spring from those basic truths which are fundamental for all ages and all experiences. He senses the meaning of the earth and her productions; of man, the final and the consummate flower, and throughout his work he expresses the interrelating unity of man with nature. He shows us Man evolving out of the beast in a struggle with another centaur; he portrays the recumbent Mother crouched against a centaur who holds the child in his arms – the child who is already one step beyond, a concept closely parallel to that of Nietzsche. In yet another picture he shows us Man driving or being driven by a horse, divinely frenzied.

His centaurs and horses have a charm beyond their natures so that they are never wholly animal in character. They have a grace which is reminiscent of the Chinese statuettes of horses, with their square nostrils and delicate hoofs, hoofs that paw the air rather than the ground and stamp upon the mind the finest qualities of a horse, its fleetness, swiftness and strength. So that in regarding these centaurs we sense the beast that is yet man and again that man which is and must be animal; we become conscious of that evolution upwards which is in itself a miracle, although there is a barrier which will for ever prevent man from clutching the stars.

The picture of the flying figure suggests the sweeping onrush of the winged victory, man's supreme aspiration; it is symbol of the divine force which impels man for ever onward to higher levels of evolution. The study of the human body in flight has been a source of inspiration to almost every artist; in the Palazzo Ducale at Venice for instance,

Tintoretto has introduced a multitude of flying figures into his great ceiling painting of 'Venice as the Queen of the Adriatic'. But in all these studies there are certain distortions of the human body. These forms are either too aspirant or too convulsive so that one is unpleasantly reminded of the muscular sensations of cramped arms and benumbed legs.

In the Sistine Chapel however, the great patriarchal paintings of the Jehovah creating the world, dividing the waters of the earth or sweeping through space to touch the finger of the recumbent Adam, are all so balanced and so benignly reposeful that they convey not only a sense of flight through space but the impression of the very weight of space which is able to sustain these moving bodies.

Gibran's studies of movement are akin to those of Michelangelo because he has arrived at a unity of thought and representation. Not only is he the master of the symbolic idea which he expresses but he has attained the technical grasp upon his material. Hence we are not disconcerted by false concepts of the human body or erroneous perspectives.

His paintings are mostly wash drawings and only here and there does his pencil co-operate with his brush to suggest and complete the theme. The level of his painting is very delicate – plane suggesting another plane in the most subtle gradation so that at first there seems to be but little colour and then comes a swift realization that it is all colour – only imperceptibly diffused. In one or two of the studies like the sombre picture of the man with the cap, more vivid reds and blues are introduced and a certain greenish blue, wholly of the East, reappears constantly in his studies of definite types. But in his more profound interpretative work, the gradation of colour is delicate in the extreme. He uses colour to reveal his form, unlike many painters who lose their sense of form in the pursuit of colour; that is another reason why his paintings are so suggestive of the art of the sculptor.

This impression is conveyed most powerfully in the study of a woman's head, the frontispiece to this volume, a painting which is the most complete exposition of the art of Gibran. Her head is thrown back and seems to rest upon a white background that is yet not exactly white; it is the colour of the sea at an infinite distance when colour is no longer colour but merely light. The head, lying upon this luminous ground is so delicately delineated that the throat veins almost quiver and the pale lips are about to move. And as we look upon the fine profile, the sensitive, highly arched nose and the tender, compassionate mouth, it seems as if this woman's head had arisen out of those deeper waters which we call the sea of memory, as if indeed 'Our souls have sight of that immortal sea from whence we came'.

There is little drawing as we are accustomed to think of drawing but the painting is modelled in colour and is akin to the interpretation of a sculptor who usually seeks the greater freedom which larger material begets. That something flowing which alone makes the earth other than a piece of stone is revealed in almost all his work. It is the very soul of sculpture and he is but expressing it in kindred form.

Gibran is an interpreter of 'the heavens above and the earth below'. He recalls like a fleeting memory, the meaning of the great clouds which swept like a flock of storm gulls before the bewildered eyes of primitive man, but he has likewise sounded the pit of agony into which the soul descends during the crucifixion of its development. For Gibran is not alone interested in the history of life; he is not concerned merely with its portrayal, he shares its struggle. He is impelled by that force which lies beyond all things animate and inanimate – that force which produces, destroys and recreates with the same intensity, the same purpose and always to his eyes, with the same succession of beauty.

Therein lies the reason why his work is of today with its unrest and grouping in spite of its intuitive simplicity in the use of symbolic material of the past. It is of today because we are seeking to infuse a new meaning into life whereby we can accept the bitter in order to gain the sweet; we are endeavouring to come to terms with the ancient symbols and although the concepts which Gibran portrays are as old as Cronos, they are also as modern as the interpretative spirit of our age. His art arises out of the past but its appeal is to the thinking minds of today and it foreshadows a trend in the creative work of the future.

The triptych of the crucifixion in this series of drawings shows at once how the symbol of Christ between the two thieves can be used either to express the complete religious and mythological concept, as it would have been used by the Primitives in some large fresco, and how the same idea can be conveyed on a small sheet of paper by one who understands the inner meaning and is able to put it forth as a representation of the conflict of every self-conscious being. In this drawing a man rests upon the shoulders of two companions. There are no

religious accessories either of halo or stigmata with which to associate or localize the concept and yet the story of the crucifixion is completely portrayed.

It is in this absolute simplicity of idea and intuitive revelation coupled with an instinctive grasp of the beauty of form, that Gibran attains the consummation of his powers and commands a respect meritorious of the classic. For amidst the deluge which has overwhelmed our world of art, when Cubists collide with Vorticists and both are submerged by the onrushing of the Orphicists – when school and type arise and as swiftly decline in the quest of the new and the age is seeking a picture of its soul in barbaric imitation of genuine barbarism, it is of inestimable value to come upon an artist who is fulfilling himself in his work apart from any claptrap of modern devices. Gibran has not gone to strange lands to study the new but he has walked the silent path of the meditative creator and he has brought out of his own depths these eternal verities of the history of man's inner life. He has recreated the symbolic incarnation of the All-Mother – he has divined the flying wish of humanity and he has lain bare and retold the story of the Passion.

In the poetic revelation of these psychological concepts of humanity he exhibits a world of consummate beauty to the younger artists of America whose life he has chosen to share. He is expressing the vast, the infinite forms of the ever fluid past and is showing us how these imperishable memories can stimulate the art of the future.

Only in the acceptance of this infinitely varied racial history as a living part of the present, will America prepare herself for the eventual renaissance of the arts and as a forerunner of this renaissance, Gibran will occupy a similar position to that of Giotto and Ghirlandaio in rela-tion to the Italian Golden Age. The painters of the Renaissance showed the world that the human being could be portrayed as if he were divine. But to those who preceded the Renaissance the 'as if' did not exist. To them – as to Gibran, human life is divine. The body reflects and represents the spirit, and art arises out of the interplay between the inner and the outer world.

It is a fact that in painting as well as in poetry, we are standing today on the tiptoes of expectation, awaiting the fusion of a closer union between the old world and the new. We are no longer bounded by New England concepts of the poetical on the one side and by the various quasi-tragic representations of the Last of the Mohicans as a basic expression of American art on the other. In the anticipation of the eventual renaissance of the world, we in America can lend ourselves to study those who are its precursors.

For Gibran belongs to that group of artists whose message always heralds a period of transition and whose voice challenges the present to a recapitulation of its standards.

There is a tradition so old that its origin is lost in the mists of antiquity where it is acclaimed as the symbol of our common ancestor Adam. Its sign signifies 'Dum voluit spiritus Mundi'. Out of the illimitable past – illuminating the East, touching in turn Greece, Italy, Flanders, Germany, France and Spain – so passed the great creative spirit in the world of art; what if this same illuminative spirit should be in turn approaching our shores, provided that we are receptive enough to understand and to assimilate its fundamental message.

EPILOGUE

My spirit is to me a companion who comforts me when the days grow heavy upon me; who consoles me when the afflictions of life multiply.

Who is not a companion to his spirit is an enemy to people. And he who seems not in his self a friend dies despairing. For life springs from within a man and comes not from without him.

I came to say a word and I shall utter it. Should death take me ere I give voice, the morrow shall utter it. For the morrow leaves not a secret hidden in the book of the Infinite.

I came to live in the splendour of Love and the light of Beauty.

Behold me then in life; people cannot separate me from my life.

Should they put out my eyes I would listen to the songs of love and the melodies of beauty and gladness. Were they to stop my ears I would find joy in the caress of the breeze compounded of beauty's fragrance and the sweet breaths of lovers.

And if I am denied the air I will live with my spirit; for the spirit is the daughter of love and beauty.

I came to be for all and in all. That which alone I do today shall be proclaimed before the people in days to come. And what I now say with one tongue, tomorrow will say with many.

Kahlil Gibran
From *A Tear and a Smile*
Translated by H M Nahmad

BIBLIOGRAPHY

The following are the sources from which all the quotations in this anthology have been extracted. All references are listed in the order in which the passages appear in each section.

Selections from Gibran's Arabic works in translation

Al-Musiqah (Music):

Passage is from *The Voice of the Master*, translated from the Arabic by Anthony R Ferris (London: Heinemann, 1973), pp. 57–58.

'Ara'is al-Muruj (Nymphs of the Valley):

Passage is from *Nymphs of the Valley*, translated from the Arabic by H M Nahmad (London: Heinemann, 1961), pp. 18–33.

Al-'Arwah al-Mutamarridah (Spirits Rebellious):

Passage is translated directly from the Arabic by the Editor.

Al-'Ajniha al-Mutakassirah (The Broken Wings):

Passages are taken from *The Broken Wings*, translated from the Arabic by Anthony R Ferris (New York: The Citadel Press, 1957), pp. 51, 77–78, 87, 92, 104–105, 113.

Dam'ah wa Ibtisamah (A Tear and a Smile):

Passages are taken from *A Tear and a Smile*, translated from the Arabic by H M Nahmad (London: Heinemann, 1972), pp. 27–29, 87–88,

163–164; *Prose Poems*, translated from the Arabic by Andrew Ghareeb (London: Heinemann, 1972), pp. 29–42, 63–68. The last two passages are translated directly from the Arabic by the Editor.

Al-Mawakib (The Processions):

Passages are taken from *The Processions*, translated from the Arabic by George Kheirallah (New York: The Wisdom Library, 1958), pp. 37, 39, 71–74.

Al-'Awasif (The Tempests):

Passages are taken from *A Treasury of Kahlil Gibran*, edited by Martin L Wolf and translated from the Arabic by Anthony Rizcallah Ferris (New York: The Citadel Press, 1965), pp. 339–345; *Prose Poems*, pp. 3–11, 12–15, 55–62.

Al-Badayi' wa al-Taray'if (Beautiful and Rare Sayings):

Passages are taken from *Prose Poems*, pp. 21–28, 43–54, 75, 76–77; *A Treasury of Kahlil Gibran*, pp. 139, 140; *Thoughts and Meditations*, translated from the Arabic and edited by Anthony R Ferris (New York: The Citadel Press, 1969), pp. 115–116. The last passage is translated directly from the Arabic by the Editor.

Selections from Gibran's English works

From *The Madman: his parables and poems* (London: Heinemann, 1971), pp. 7–8, 41, 46, 71–73.

From *The Forerunner: his parables and poems* (London: Heinemann, 1972), pp. 7–8, 29, 37, 39–40, 46.

From *The Prophet* (New York: Alfred A Knopf, 1998), pp. 15–16, 17–18, 50–51.

From *Sand and Foam* (London: Heinemann, 1954), pp. 1–14, 21, 23, 25.

From *Jesus, the Son of Man: His words and His deeds as told and recorded by those who knew Him* (London: Heinemann, 1969), pp. 11–14, 71–72.

From *The Earth Gods* (London: Heinemann, 1969), pp. 6–8, 40–41.

From *The Wanderer: his parables and his sayings* (London: Heinemann, 1972), pp. 3–4, 30–31, 77–78, 88–89.

From *The Garden of the Prophet* (London: Heinemann, 1972), pp. 10, 48–50.

Three Lebanese folk poems translated from the Arabic by Gibran

From *The Syrian World*, Volume I, March 1927; Volume I, May 1927; Volume II, August 1927.

Selections from the letters

Miscellaneous letters

From *A Self-Portrait*, translated from the Arabic and edited by Anthony R Ferris (New York: The Citadel Press, 1969).

Letters to Ameen Rihani

From *Unpublished Gibran Letters to Ameen Rihani*, translated with an introduction by Suheil Badi Bushrui (Beirut: World Lebanese Cultural Union, 1972).

Letters to May Ziadah

From *Love Letters: the love letters of Kahlil Gibran to May Ziadah*, translated and edited by Suheil Bushrui and Salma Haffar al-Kuzbari (Oxford: Oneworld, 1999).

Letters to Mary Haskell

From *Beloved Prophet: The love letters of Kahlil Gibran and Mary Haskell and her private journal*, edited and arranged by Virginia Hilu (New York: Alfred A. Knopf, 1972).

Others on Gibran

Gibran: the man

From *Beloved Prophet*; from C F Bragdon, 'Modern Prophet from Lebanon,' in *Merely Players* (New York: Alfred A Knopf, 1929); from 'Juliet Remembers Gibran' in Marzieh Gail, *Other People, Other Places* (Oxford: George Ronald, 1982); from Barbara Young *This Man from Lebanon: A Study of Kahlil Gibran* (New York: Alfred A Knopf, 1945).

Gibran: the poet:

The Living Torch, from George Russell (New York: Macmillan and Co., 1938); from Khalil S Hawi *Kahlil Gibran: His Background, Character and Works* (Beirut: American University of Beirut, 1963); from Robert Hillyer, 'Introduction' to *A Tear and a Smile*, translated from the Arabic by H M Nahmad (London: Heinemann, 1972); from Mikhail Naimy: A variation, and not an accurate translation, of the address in Arabic at the opening of the Gibran International Festival, 1970. The text of Mr. Naimy's piece has been left precisely as he translated it himself from Arabic into English [Editor]; Francis Warner's poem 'For Bisharri', composed in Gibran's hometown, summer 1970; from Aïcha Lemsine Laïdi, Tribute published in the brochure, 'An Evening for Gibran: Gala Dinner' (London: 19 November 1991); Kathleen Raine, 'Foreword' to Suheil Bushrui and Joe Jenkins' *Kahlil Gibran. Man and Poet, a new biograhy* (Oxford: Oneworld, 1998).

Gibran: the artist:

From Yusuf Huwayyik, *Gibran in Paris*, translated and with an introduction by Matti Moosa (New York: Popular Library, 1976); From Alice Raphael, 'Introduction' to Kahlil Gibran's *Twenty Drawings* (New York: Alfred A Knopf, 1919).

ACKNOWLEDGEMENTS

Acknowledgement is hereby extended to Alfred A Knopf, Inc., a division of Random House, Inc., for permission to reprint material from the following books by Kahlil Gibran:

The Madman: copyright 1918 by Kahlil Gibran. Renewal copyright 1946 by Administrators C T A of Kahlil Gibran Estate and Mary G Gibran · *The Forerunner*: copyright 1920 by Kahlil Gibran. Renewal copyright 1948 by Administrators C T A of Kahlil Gibran Estate and Mary G Gibran · *The Prophet*: copyright 1923 by Kahlil Gibran. Renewal copyright 1951 by Administrators C T A of Kahlil Gibran Estate and Mary G Gibran · *Sand and Foam*: copyright 1926 by Kahlil Gibran. Renewal copyright 1954 by Administrators C T A of Kahlil Gibran Estate and Mary G Gibran · *Jesus, the Son of Man*: copyright 1928 by Kahlil Gibran. Renewal copyright 1956 by Administrators C T A of Kahlil Gibran Estate and Mary G Gibran · *The Earth Gods*: copyright 1931 by Kahlil Gibran. Renewal copyright 1959 by Administrators C T A of Kahlil Gibran Estate and Mary G Gibran · *The Wanderer*: copyright 1932 by Kahlil Gibran. Renewal copyright 1960 by Administrators C T A of Kahlil Gibran Estate and Mary G Gibran · *The Garden of the Prophet*: copyright 1933 by Alfred A Knopf, Inc. Renewal copyright 1961 by Mary G Gibran · *Twenty Drawings*: copyright 1919 by Alfred A Knopf, Inc. Renewal copyright 1947 by Administrators C T A of Kahlil Gibran

Estate and Mary G Gibran · *A Tear and a Smile*: copyright 1950 by Alfred A Knopf, Inc. · *Nymphs of the Valley*: copyright 1948 by Alfred A Knopf, Inc. · *Beloved Prophet*: copyright 1972 by Alfred A Knopf, Inc. · *Prose Poems*: copyright 1934 by Alfred A Knopf, Inc. · *Spirits Rebellious*: copyright 1948 by Alfred A Knopf, Inc.

and for permission to reprint from the following books:

Merely Players: copyright 1929 by C F Bragdon · *This Man from Lebanon*: copyright 1945 by Barbara Young

Acknowledgement is also extended to the following publishers and holders of copyright:

Alfred A Knopf, Inc. for Robert Hillyer's introduction to *A Tear and a Smile* · Anthony R Ferris for extracts from *Thoughts and Meditations*: copyright 1960 · S B Bushrui and Salma Haffar al-Kuzbari for extracts from *Love Letters*: copyright 1983, 1995, 1999 · The Citadel Press for extracts from *The Broken Wings, Kahlil Gibran: A Self-Portrait, A Treasury of Kahlil Gibran, The Voice of the Master* · Dr Khalil S Hawi for his conclusion to *Kahlil Gibran: His Background, Character and Works* · Mrs. G Kheirallah for extracts from *The Procession* · Mr Mikhail Naimy for extracts from *Kahlil Gibran: His Life and his Work* · George Ronald Publisher Limited for extracts from *Other People, Other Places* · Colin Smythe Limited on behalf of the heirs of Diarmuid Russell for extracts from *The Living Torch* · The poet Francis Warner for his poem, 'For Bisharri'.

Please note that every effort has been made to trace and acknowledge ownership of copyright. If any required credits have been omitted or any rights overlooked, it is completely unintentional.